UNDERSTANDING THE LOVE OF GOD IN CHURCH HURT: *It's Time to Heal!*

UNDERSTANDING THE LOVE OF GOD IN CHURCH HURT: *It's Time to Heal!*

Prophetess Evangelist
Fern Yvette Harris, PhD

All Scripture quotations are from the King James Version of the Bible.

All definitions marked (MWCD) are from the Merriam-Webster collegiate dictionary®, (11th ed.), (1995). Spring-field, MA: Merriam-Webster.

All Hebrew and Greek definitions marked (S.C.) are from The New Strong's Exhaustive Concordance of the Bible, Copyright © 1990 by Thomas Nelson Publishers

All definitions marked (Vines) are from the Vine's Complete Expository Dictionary of Old and New Testament Words, Copyright © 1985, by Thomas Nelson Publishers

"Understanding the Love of God in Church Hurt: It's Time to Heal!" by Prophetess Evangelist Fern Yvette Harris, PhD

Cover illustration inspired by the *Holy Ghost:* Prophetess Evangelist Fern Yvette Harris, PhD

Published by: Prophetess Evangelist Fern Yvette Harris, PhD
4980 S. Alma School Road
Ste. A2, #259
Chandler, AZ 85248
www.ATcicJMinistries.org

ISBN 978-0-578-31354-2
Copyright © 2020, 2021 by Prophetess Evangelist Fern Yvette Harris, PhD
Printed in the United States of America

I dedicate this book to those dearly beloved by the LORD. If you believe in Jesus Christ and are experiencing a struggle, test, or trial, the LORD loves you. Endure to the end, never giving up no matter what you go through, and you shall receive the Kingdom of Heaven!

"For whom the Lord loveth he chasteneth, and scourgeth every son whom he receiveth. If ye endure chastening, God dealeth with you as with sons; for what son is he whom the father chasteneth not?"

Hebrews 12:6-7

The Lord Jesus told me to add this statement to the book:
Although I hold a PhD, *this book is written in Biblical language* and not an academic language.
I am the Lord's Minister first. Hallelujah!
God bless you.

TABLE OF CONTENTS

PREFACE

Many believers in the Body of Christ think once they give their life to Jesus Christ, they will experience a cakewalk from Earth to Heaven. The Lord promised us the Holy Ghost as a comforter to strengthen and guide us on our journey, yet He never promised a trouble-free walk. The truth is we all must endure suffering to enter into the Kingdom of Heaven (2nd Timothy 3:12). Our gracious Abba, Father in Heaven, sent His only begotten Son, Jesus Christ, to be the door of salvation to all who will believe His Son's testimony. Sadly, the way to eternal life is not a well-trodden road. The Bible declares in Matthew 7:14, *"Because strait is the gate, and narrow is the way, which leadeth unto life, and few there be that find it."*

Why would millions of people who believe Jesus Christ came to die for our sins fail to receive the Kingdom of Heaven? The answer is simple: They will refuse to forgive. It's unbelievable, yet it is true. Although we have freely and abundantly received forgiveness for our sins, many will miss the Kingdom of Heaven because they will not forgive others. The Book of Mark 11:25-26 cautions, *"And when ye stand praying, forgive, if ye have ought against any: that your Father also which is in heaven may forgive you your trespasses. But if ye do not forgive, neither will your Father which is in heaven forgive your trespasses."* This book admonishes readers who desire to move forward in their walk with the Lord to forgive those who injured them.

EXPLANATION OF FRONT BOOK COVER

One day, while I was walking and praying, the Lord showed me the front cover of this book. I used simply drawing tools to start putting the Church House together. Over a period of time, He added more details on the Church and told me: *My Church is split. The doctrine that many Churches are operating in is not sound. Therefore, many of my children, whom I love dearly, are misled by false teachers and ministers. The world is using this opportunity while the Church is divided to cause the Church to fade in the background. But! The Body of Christ shall come forth greater than ever. I will purge my floor of all those who are hindering my Church from moving forward. Those operating in sound doctrine, the foundational part of the picture, will go forth to correct the Church throughout the world, and they shall endure until the end and shall receive Eternal Life. The top part of the picture will be broken off and cast into everlasting fire because they refuse to repent!*

The Bible declares, *"Knowing this first, that there shall come in the last days scoffers, walking after their own lusts,"* (2nd Peter 3:3). Scoffers in the S.C. 1703 in the Greek means: a derider that is a false teacher; a mocker. A derider laughs and insults the Lord's anointed. They subject the children of God to bitter and contemptuous ridicule and criticism. They often express a lack of respect or approval toward the Lord's true Apostles, Prophets, and Prophetesses.

Also, 2nd Timothy 4:3-5 a-only gives a strong warning: *"For the time will come when they will not endure sound doctrine; but after their own lusts shall they heap to themselves teachers, having itching ears; And they shall turn away their ears from the truth, and shall be turned into fables. But watch thou in all things,"*

"And I will bring the third part through the fire, and will refine them as silver is refined, and will try them as gold is tried: they shall call on my name, and I will hear them: I will say, It is my people: and they shall say, The LORD is my God" (Zechariah 13:9).

ACKNOWLEDGMENTS

I genuinely give all praise, honor, and glory to the Lord Jesus Christ, my Lord and Savior, for never leaving me. Lord, You reminded me I belong to You. There were times I nearly lost my mind, but it was Your hand upon my life for good that kept me. You gave me many Psalms and a greater anointing to understand the power of forgiveness. I thank You for being my stay and strength, even when I did not know You.

To my husband, Michealangelo Harris, the love of my life: *"Iron sharpeneth iron; so a man sharpeneth the countenance of his friend"* (Proverbs 27:17). Thank you for all your insight, words of wisdom, and instruction concerning many chapters of this book. I longed for us to get to this place of understanding why the Lord did all that He did in both of our lives. The Lord Jesus is good!

To my most dearest and most beloved sons, Christopher and Chrison, you know how I feel. I cannot believe you have grown to be a blessing to me. I thank the Lord for the opportunity to raise you. May the Lord look upon you at this moment, remember your labor of love toward His Kingdom, and never remove His compassion and mercy. In Jesus' name.

Last but not least, I thank all of the ATcicJ Ministries disciples for your feedback on the book and support over the years. May the Lord God bless you all with *Eternal Life.* In Jesus' name.

INTRODUCTION

The Bible declares in Ephesians 6:12, *"For we wrestle not against flesh and blood, but against principalities, against powers, against the rulers of the darkness of this world, against spiritual wickedness in high places."* Although we have Scripture, many believers ignore its truths and hold relentless grudges against other people. Of a reality, worldwide, people, in general, operate in unforgivingness. Yet, what if you found out demonic forces devised most of your adversity? How would you feel knowing the adversary was the reason for many of your struggles in the Church? Would you still blame humans?

What if the adversary caused a situation in your life to test your ability to forgive? He is aware the Lord will not forgive you if you do not pardon those who sin against you. Matthew 6:14-15 declares, *"For if ye forgive men their trespasses, your heavenly Father will also forgive you: But if ye forgive not men their trespasses, neither will your Father forgive your trespasses."* The adversary desires to devour us, and he will use our human emotions and shortcomings to accomplish his goal. Therefore, the Lord instructs us to be sober and vigilant. The enemy intends to swallow us up or gulp us entirely. He attempts to drown or flood us with unforgivingness, anger, hatred, sorrows, and bitterness so we will not perceive, neither experience, the love of God nor the power of forgiveness.

The Book of Job, chapters one and two, clearly show Satan's active plan in Job's life. Moreover, Satan was actively using Peter to tempt Jesus (Matthew 16:22-23). *"And the Lord said, Simon, Simon, behold, Satan hath desired to have you, that he may sift you as wheat: But I have prayed for thee, that thy faith fail not: and when thou art converted, strengthen thy brethren"* (Luke 22:31-32). The adversary is present in many Scriptures. It was Satan who entered Judas Iscariot in the betrayal of Jesus (John 13:27). And it was Satan who tried to tempt Jesus in the wilderness (Luke 4:1-14).

You see, I believe there was a devilish influence that urged King Herod to order the death of Jesus upon His birth (Matthew 2:16). I believe the same evil influence provoked Pharaoh's attempt to annihilate the Hebrew boys under two years old in Moses' day (Exodus 1:15-16, 22). I know it was not the Lord because the Lord rewarded the midwives who refused to obey Pharaoh (Exodus 1:17-21). Moreover, I know it is not the Lord aborting millions of babies around the world today. Satan provokes humans to do the evil they do, and the Lord allows it because humans have hardened their hearts against God. *"And even as they did not like to retain God in their knowledge, God gave them over to a reprobate mind, to do those things which are not convenient;"* (Romans 1:28).

Understand, it was the evil in the era's religious leaders that caused them to crucify the Messiah. However, they did not know that God the Father, in His infinite wisdom, knew what they would do and planned to turn the crucifixion of an innocent man into a holy sacrifice to atone for the sins of the whole world. That's what the Lord does. He takes the enemy's plans and turns them around for our good like he did at the end of Job's trial. Job maintained his integrity and saw the glory of the Lord (Job 42). Oh! I know the Lord does orchestrate many things because He creates good and evil (Isaiah 45:7). However, I do not believe it is the Lord plotting against His children to fail. He does not have to conspire and scheme to cause you to fail. He can think of your failure, and it happens. What He does do is tailor-make lessons in life to renew our minds and build our character.

This book addresses believers who struggle to forgive those in the Church who caused them significant pain and suffering. It gives detailed accounts of different types of Church hurt and how to overcome the pain associated with congregation life. Believers who have read this book said it made them feel all kinds of emotions and brought back deeply rooted injuries. After completing the review, they expressed how they received healing and understanding of how to handle future injuries. As you read this book, you will feel freedom from bondage. You will also gain an understanding of your situation and begin to forgive. As you forgive, you will experience healing in the depths of your soul. Do not think of this book as a form of entertainment, but see it as a spiritual journey where you experience the love of God and His healing power. Utilize this book as a tool to assist you in loving those around you more deeply. God bless you!

CHAPTER ONE

THE POWER OF FORGIVENESS

"And forgive us our debts, as we forgive our debtors."

Matthew 6:12

CHAPTER 1: *THE POWER OF FORGIVENESS*

"For his anger endureth but a moment; in his favour is life: weeping may endure for a night, but joy cometh in the morning" Psalm 30:5. As I write this chapter, I can honestly say the Lord has given me an understanding of why I went through the things I have gone through over the last sixteen years. Onlookers of my plight have said, "Wow, you went through all of that? I couldn't have done it. I wouldn't have done it." Yes, I had to go through all of that so I could have a new mindset.

I know you are thinking: "What did she go through?" I experienced everything I thought or said I would never do or tolerate. I went through all of the things I put my mind on when others were going through life experiences. It wasn't every instance of life, just some specific things that I deemed unacceptable. If I had judged it at some point in my life, I went through a trial to show me the error in my thinking concerning that thing. If I felt strongly about something and someone tried to tell me otherwise, and I didn't listen, the Lord allowed me to experience that very thing to show me what they were trying to say to me; he also showed me why people responded the way they did when they were in their situation.

I will not indicate specifics on what I have gone through because each person is unique; what the Lord puts us through will be different in many ways, even if it is the same test. For instance, some may have to endure a situation at home or Church; some may have an illness in their body; some may suffer grief due to an unexpected loss of people, property, or livelihood. I cannot be specific because I don't know what situations the Lord has predetermined for you to go through; what I went through may not apply to you, and even if it did, we are different people, and we handle things differently. Furthermore, I don't know what you may have done that displeased the Lord. I do know that He corrected me on a range of things from every area of life. 1st Peter 4:12 declares, *"Beloved, think it not strange concerning the fiery trial which is to try you, as though some strange thing happened unto you: But rejoice, inasmuch as ye are partakers of Christ's sufferings; that, when his glory shall be revealed, ye may be glad also with exceeding joy."* Just know that whatever you have said or thought that you would not put up with is likely to be the thing the Lord will require you to endure if you desire to be saved. If the Lord loves you, He will correct your character and mindset.

Listen, most of the things I endured had to do with incorrect attitudes and some things I said to other people when I was a young lady in the world. Other things had to do with questioning if what the Lord was doing in someone else's life was right. I would see a situation and ask myself: Is that God? I had the audacity to think on the Lord's business. I must have been crazy. No one knows what the Lord is doing in others' lives. So why do we walk around judging everyone and everything when the Lord did not say anything to us concerning the matter? You've heard the phrase, "Something is not right, but I don't know what it is" or "It doesn't sit right with my spirit." I didn't necessarily use those phrases, but I foolishly questioned within myself some things that were going on with certain Church folk that had nothing to do with me. Three specific situations come to mind, and I suffered each one.

God is good! Everything the Lord put me through helped me understand that He is in complete control of human lives, saved and unsaved. It's like when you ask the Lord a question about someone else's situation, and He sends the answer by way of trial. When you are in the trial, you know it's all the Lord, yet you could not see it was the Lord before that when someone else was in the situation; a trial will open your eyes to see just how much the Lord is in everybody's life and they are not all in sin in the Lord's eyes because He is the One who orchestrated the whole thing. John 21:21-22 declares, *"Peter seeing him saith to Jesus, Lord, and what shall this man do? Jesus saith unto him, If I will that he tarry till I come, what is that to thee? follow thou me."* In other words, Jesus said, mind your own business.

What I learned the most is that our Lord, Jesus Christ, is not religious. He will subject you to some unpleasant experiences, and there is nothing anyone can do about it. When I was going through my appointed trials to perfect my character, the Lord had to humble me by subjecting me to specific things, and He used other people to bring about that perfection. And guess what, while I was trying to hold on to my sanity and salvation, people were saying, "you are in sin; you're on your way to hell; you missed it; the devil tricked you!" BUT GOD caused me to come through those things unscathed and with a lot more character, and He has still promised me salvation.

You need to understand that everyone's story has already been written and lived in the mind of God before the foundation of the world (Ephesians 1:4-6), including edits and deletes; an edit would be a name change, and a delete would be like a spouse's death in a marriage the Lord did not approve. You just have to walk out the plan of God for your life and salvation. You cannot change the Lord's plan or go around it. The Lord knows your end from the beginning (Isaiah 46:10). Besides, what the Lord put me through is unimportant because I have already endured what He required of me; more importantly, you should consider what He will require of <u>you</u> because of what <u>you</u> said, thought, or might have even done? I can tell you this, if you belong to Jesus and you endure whatever He has appointed for you, you will obtain mercy at the Judgment Seat of Christ and receive *Eternal Life.*

Regardless of how it appeared to others, each trial has genuinely fulfilled the Lord's perfect plan for my life. Now, the Lord has given me understanding, and I am not angry or bitter with anyone. I now know the Lord used every situation and circumstance to teach me many of life's lessons. And those who tried to hurt me, instead, brought to pass His plan for my life. What I learned the most is we all have the ability to make free will choices. What we do with our choice in each situation is up to us. I used my free will to choose the Lord's perfect, divine, and acceptable will for my life, and I didn't take the way of escape like so many Christians do today. 1st Corinthians 10:13 declares, *"There hath no temptation taken you but such as is common to man: but God is faithful, who will not suffer you*

7

to be tempted above that ye are able; but will with the temptation also make a way to escape, that ye may be able to bear it."

It didn't matter what the situation was I was going through; I decided to forgive and endure the pain of the test or trial. That made it easier to follow the Lord's instructions, even when it hurt, and it hurt much. Releasing pride and ignoring the evil others were saying about me was difficult, but I pressed on to do the Lord's will, no matter the cost to my reputation. I made a conscious decision to be a fool for Christ and was not concerned if others did not approve of what the Lord was doing in my life. I chose to continue on a journey with Jesus Christ, leaving everyone and everything behind, if necessary.

I can honestly say the tests I went through made my life better and more fulfilling. Yet, I had to endure the tests and trials to reap that benefit. And it seemed impossible. Although each ordeal seemed long and heart-wrenching, the Lord was there carrying me through. At the time, it seemed as if the Lord took a long time to answer my cries. However, Jesus is my help and my strength, and He faithfully delivered me out of all my troubles.

I noticed the Lord spoke to me more frequently than usual when I went through difficult situations, including a trial I encountered several years ago. During that ordeal, which now seems long ago, He always encouraged me throughout the day, telling me not to give up my inheritance. He would often say, *"Be strong and of good courage. I AM with thee. I will strengthen thee. I will prosper thee. Don't be afraid."* He told me to stay in my test and trial. He specifically said, *"Stay in the ministry where I placed you. If you endure this, there will be a blessing on the other side of it. Don't let them run you out of your inheritance."*

Humiliation can cause a person to run from a situation, but I knew if I ran, I would always be running. See, when you are going through a test or trial, the enemy's goal is to incite you to give up and depart from the will of God. However, the Lord's aim is for you to endure the test, stay in His will, and afterward experience an abundant life. If you bail out during the test, you will never taste the life the Lord has planned for you. Abiding in His will causes growth in your character. It increases your strength in your walk with the Lord. Why am I saying the test is the will of God? If the Lord allows you to go through it, then it is His will. He has the power to stop the test, so when He does not, it is His will for you to experience and go through the situation.

If you flee the test, you run from the will of God, and if you run from the will of God, then you leave God. Whether he has placed you in a Church, marriage, home, city, or nation, if you leave before He releases you, then you are out of His will. If you are not in the Lord's will, then you are in a precarious place in your walk, and only the mercy of God can keep the enemy from having his way with you. If you decide later to return to the Lord and do it His way, you will find the same test waiting on you when you return. The test will automatically pick up from where it left off. Only it will be prolonged and more intense. That is another reason I chose to endure my test.

You see, surrendering my life to the Lord Jesus Christ has been one of the most beautifully painful experiences I have encountered. Many do not understand walking with the Lord is similar to a pregnant woman travailing. It is often painful and discomforting, yet delightful, especially for those who have been waiting for a long time to bear children. It is also a mystery how, after the child is born, the mother forgets the pain and discomfort and feels astonishment.

Why is this walk in the Lord beautiful and painful at the same time? I mean, when we allow the Lord to bring us through a painful and traumatizing situation instead of retreating, we find afterward, we are renewed, mended, and healed. When the dust settles, and we look at the situation closely, we see it was only the Lord who brought us out of it and gave us great understanding, a new heart, and the right spirit. We also come to delight in knowing the purpose of the test and gladly share the experiences we once considered traumatic with others. We also receive revelation in our tests and trials by allowing the Lord to work His will in our lives. We feel grateful and are inspired to love the Lord and others more deeply. We also discover we are endowed with power from the Lord to assist others who are struggling with the same situation we came through.

So, what are these tests and trials we face in our walk with the Lord? For some, it is persecution, and for others, it consists of all the situations necessary to undergo a spiritual transformation. This transformation causes us to cease being led by our carnal nature to being led by the Holy Ghost. A spiritual test is when the Lord tries our hearts concerning a particular matter. During that test, He will require some things of all those who claim to love Him. He will expect us to show our love for Him by requiring us to make sacrifices and endure some things. Unfortunately, there is a lie about Christianity, stating that everything will be easy if you give your life to Jesus. Some even falsely promote that there is little to no suffering in Christ because Jesus already suffered for us.

On the contrary, 2nd Timothy 2:12-13 declares, *"If we suffer, we shall also reign with him: if we deny him, he also will deny us: If we believe not, yet he abideth faithful: he cannot deny himself."* Consider this Biblical example of a test tailor-made for a young man. *"And, behold, one came and said unto him, Good Master, what good thing shall I do, that I may have eternal life? And he said unto him, Why callest thou me good? there is none good but one, that is, God: but if thou wilt enter into life, keep the commandments. He saith unto him, Which? Jesus said, Thou shalt do no murder, Thou shalt not commit adultery, Thou shalt not steal, Thou shalt not bear false witness, Honour thy father and thy mother: and, Thou shalt love thy neighbour as thyself. The young man saith unto him, All these things have I kept from my youth up: what lack I yet? Jesus said unto him, If thou wilt be perfect, go and sell that thou hast, and give to the poor, and thou shalt have treasure in heaven: and come and follow me. But when the young man heard that saying, he went away sorrowful: for he had great possessions. Then said Jesus unto his disciples, Verily I say unto you, That a rich man shall hardly enter into the kingdom of heaven. And again I say unto you, It is easier for a camel to go through the eye of a needle, than for a rich man to enter into the kingdom of God"* (Matthew 19:16-24). How did the young man know he lacked something? When humans ask those kinds of questions, they know something is not right but do not desire to face the answer.

If thou will be perfect, then the Lord will require some things of you, which may prove difficult to bear. He will also use other people to bring you into your destiny. At first, it will appear as if those whom the Lord is using are coming out against you, but they are just instruments and tools to sharpen you, especially if they are in the Church. Proverbs 27:17 explains, *"Iron sharpeneth iron; so a man sharpeneth the countenance of his friend."*

Our God is a Potter, and He is always working at the Potter's wheel. The Book of Jeremiah 18:1-6 declares, *"THE word which came to Jeremiah from the LORD, saying, Arise, and go down to the potter's house, and there I will cause thee to hear my words. Then I went down to the potter's house, and, behold, he wrought a work on the wheels. And the vessel that he made of clay was marred in the hand of the potter: so he made it again another vessel, as seemed good to the potter to make it. Then the word of the LORD came to me, saying, O house of Israel, cannot I do with you as this potter? saith the LORD. Behold, as the clay is in the potter's hand, so are ye in mine hand, O house of Israel."*

The key here is the Lord is doing the reshaping and remolding, not the devil, and not the brethren whom you see as your enemies. It is the Lord! What you are going through is an opportunity for you to choose to forgive or not forgive. The peace I have today results from yielding to the Holy Spirit and His instruction to forgive others. And I believe peace will increase as I continue to walk in the power of forgiveness.

Believe me. I know what it feels like to have no peace. Before I gave my life to Jesus, I was in a place of unforgivingness. What I noticed was that I became angry, short-tempered, critical, and downright ugly. The more people hurt me, the worse I became. I was relentless in my efforts to let everyone know about my pain. I even told people at work who knew nothing of those I slandered. I gained a lot of pity. However, I did not know my heart grew darker as I ran my mouth. There was one person who hurt me who could not come into my presence without getting cussed out. I would see them coming and just start railing on them so bad they would just put their head down. They never responded or retaliated. Unforgivingness was eating me up inside. That went on for five years. Even though it seemed I was prospering, I was not. I was stagnated by unforgivingness in many areas of my life. I was miserable, and it showed because I was hostile and aggressive. I snapped at people all the time, and I did not realize it a lot of times.

Then I gave my life to Jesus. He instructed me right away to forgive the primary person who hurt me. I immediately complied with the Lord, and He opened a door for me to speak with the person so they would know I forgave them. As we talked, I experienced an unbelievable peace in my mind and soul. I calmed, and bitterness left me. The person also felt a release after being forgiven. As we both wept, the person explained they never meant to hurt me. Life happened, and things just spiraled out of their control. Now, after two decades, we still have a peaceable relationship.

Although the Lord had given me peace concerning that person, I was still a work in progress. Another thing that happened was I began to see where I, too, had hurt others, and I desired to make it right. There was one person in particular whom I needed to repent to, but we lost touch. I did not know how to contact them to make it right, so I prayed and asked the Lord to allow me to get it right with the person. Years passed after I prayed that prayer, then the person called my home. It was right on time, too, because I was getting ready to move, and my landline phone number would change. I was so thankful they called that I immediately began to repent and ask for their forgiveness. Their response to me was not welcoming. They immediately said, "Yeah, you used to . . . ." They began to remind me of all the things I used to do to them. I held my peace. I did not think or say anything. I asked for forgiveness again, and we ended the conversation. Although I tried to rectify the situation, I do not believe they forgave me. However, my conscience was clear. After I settled those matters, I noticed I could forgive and ask for forgiveness more readily. I also became stronger in my walk with the Lord.

There are no perfect people in the world or any Church. As much as we would like to believe there are faultless people in our Church, it is just not true. Even Church leaders have weaknesses in their character. It is so important to have prayer and true Bible doctrine in the Church. Only then will people be more inclined to spirituality rather than carnality and fleshly desires. The Word of God admonishes, *"And blessed is he, whosoever shall not be offended in me"* Matthew 11:6.

Christians are always looking for ways to feel encouraged and to feel good about their relationship with the Lord. Many are looking for a warm and fuzzy feeling. However, without suffering and persecution, how will we learn obedience? How can we possibly comprehend forgiveness without persecution? How are we to understand the mercy of God, His compassion, and His pity if we do not suffer? How can we experience unconditional love if others do not injure us? How else would we discover humility and experience a deeper side of the Lord if we do not endure tests and trials? Through suffering, we gain an anointing? Abba, Father, gave Jesus all power AFTER He suffered (Matthew 28:18). When we go through pain and suffering, we receive power through Jesus Christ to help others.

When I mention Church in this book, I'm not talking about the "catholic organization." I'm talking about the true Church, the Body of Christ, the Ekklesia. Those who are the Ekklesia will follow the Scriptures to resolve issues in the Church and daily life. The Ekklesia will operate in love and overcome evil with good (Romans 12:21). When I say Church, I'm also identifying the location or building where the Ekklesia fellowships. In that place are sinners who do not desire to surrender their lives to Jesus. Yet, they enjoy connecting with the saints and benefiting from the outpouring of the Lord's anointing. Also, in that place are those who are religious and those who are ungodly.

Religious people refuse to operate by the Holy Ghost's power. And, the ungodly have rejected the ways of the Lord. However, neither will leave a Holy Ghost-filled Church because the religious must keep up a façade. And the ungodly seek to hold on to relationships with others in the Church. Religious and ungodly people suspect they will not receive eternal life. So the devil uses them to stir up all manner of hell in the Church. The enemy designs those hellish situations to keep other people from going to Heaven. *"But woe unto you, scribes and Pharisees, hypocrites! for ye shut up the kingdom of heaven against men: for ye neither go in yourselves, neither suffer ye them that are entering to go in* (Matthew 23:13).

Nonetheless, does it matter that the Lord is using those in the Church to build your character? Will you accept He will use whatever means He chooses? I would rather the Church be a part of the process because the Church will be more forgiving than the world. Some in the Church will also pray and fast for you throughout the process, especially when things become unsettling or hard to understand. There is not one situation I have gone through in my walk with the Lord that has not shaped and molded my heart and moved me into the proper place and position in the Lord.

The Vines defines the heart as the unseen fountains of one's private life and is the place where sin resides. The heart rests locked away within, comprises the invisible inner man (who you really are), and embodies the real character while concealing it. Simply put, the heart is your character, as my husband teaches. The Bible declares in Jeremiah 17:9, *"The heart is deceitful above all things, and desperately wicked: who can know it?"* The very nature of humans is deceitful, so only the Lord knows a person's character. Psalms 51:5-7 also declares, *"Behold, I was shapen in iniquity; and in sin did my mother conceive me. Behold, thou desirest truth in the inward parts: and in the hidden part thou shalt make me to know wisdom. Purge me with hyssop, and I shall be clean: wash me, and I shall be whiter than snow."* Yes. The Lord desires those who belong to Him to worship Him in spirit and truth (John 4:24), so He absolutely must try our hearts. He absolutely will try our character. King David said, *"Search me, O God, and know my heart: try me, and know my thoughts: And see if there be any wicked way in me, and lead me in the way everlasting"* (Psalm 139:23-24).

The depiction of human nature can be seen and experienced in everyday life, and it is depraved. We need the Blood of Jesus and its healing power to make us a new creature. *"Therefore if any man be in Christ, he is a new creature: old things are passed away; behold, all things are become new"* (2nd Corinthians 5:17). Consider the movie *Runaway Train* (Konchalovsky, 1985, 01:29:00-01:37:00), where two fugitives and a female stowaway traveled through Alaska on a

19

crewless runaway locomotive. Near the end of the film, the elder offender sent the younger fugitive outside to stop the train. However, the young man was too weary, injured, cold, and unable to accomplish the task, but the older fugitive would not accept defeat and refused to let him inside.

Fearing the young man would die, the girl yells for the older man to stop pressing him and allow him to come out of the weather: "You'll kill him!" Once he retreats, the older man beats him, telling him to get back out there and finish the job. She yells for him to leave the young man alone and says to the older fugitive, "You're an animal!" He replies, "No! Worse! Human! Human!" I thought the last line was the highlight of the movie. What could a person possibly have experienced in life to cause him to lose all compassion for other humans? What could bring him to the point of having no regard for others? Animalistic behavior is instinctive. It's consistent and predictable. However, when it comes to humans, we can choose our behavioral response, and too often, it is self-serving and unforgiving.

After the two fugitives fight almost to the death with the girl ranting to the younger, "Kill him, kill him, kill him, kill him!" They stopped fighting, released their weapons, and the scene calmed. Then the young man said, "I thought you were my friend. I thought we were partners. You were a hero to all of us." At that moment, the young man was heartbroken. *"But Jesus did not commit himself unto them, because he knew all men, And needed not that any should testify of man: for he knew what was in man"* (John 2:24-25). We can only expect humans to be and do no more than what human nature will allow: self-preservation. And if the Lord does not remove our stony heart and give us a fleshly heart, self-preservation will prevail and continue to govern all of our actions.

Now I ask you, is the damage done by the one who offended you forgivable? Yes, it is forgivable. Now, after many years, I understand the greater the measure of the Holy Ghost a person has, the more love they will have, and the more love a person has, the more they will forgive. The more they forgive, the more they are forgiven, and the more they are forgiven, the more they will love the Lord. Furthermore, someone who acknowledges they have received forgiveness for great sins against the Lord is more apt to forgive. People who do not acknowledge the saving grace of the Lord are prone to talk about someone who offended them. They are more apt to forget how far the Lord brought them. When we acknowledge the work Jesus did on the cross, we are thankful to be an heir of salvation.

Forgiveness is an excellent display of God's love for humans. Therefore, as His children, we ought to display that same love toward others and forgive their trespasses against us. Luke 7:47-48 teaches, *"Wherefore I say unto thee, Her sins, which are many, are forgiven; for she loved much: but to whom little is forgiven, the same loveth little. And he said unto her, Thy sins are forgiven."* Please understand, unforgivingness is wickedness before the Lord (Matthew 18:23-35). However, a person who has a forgiving spirit is willing to forgive. They seek to resolve a matter instead of holding on to the offense. They also allow room for people to make mistakes or falter due to weaknesses in character. A forgiving person is compassionate, so they have a genuine concern for the other party and desires to see them prosper. So, let's pray for a forgiving spirit.

Reader, beware. After you have forgiven and forgotten the trespass, evil spirits will attempt to incite you to mentally relive the situation. For instance, say you wake up in the morning and go to the bathroom to wash your face before getting into devotion, and suddenly you have a thought about something that happened to you in the past. Your first response is Huh? Why am I thinking about that? You are not. It is an evil spirit causing the thought. All you need to do is rebuke those thoughts and that spirit in the name of Jesus Christ.

22

Reader, pray this prayer with me:

Abba, Father, in the name of Jesus Christ of Nazareth, search my heart and declare to me all the error of my ways. As I read this book, reveal to me all those whom I have not forgiven. Grant me mercy to get through this book and the power to forgive. And after I forgive, grant me to forget the past so that I may move forward in You Lord, in Jesus' name. Amen. Hallelujah! Hallelujah! Hallelujah!

CHAPTER TWO

MY SOUL, WHY ART THOU CAST DOWN?

"For his anger endureth but a moment; in his favour is life: weeping may endure for a night, but joy cometh in the morning."

Psalm 30:5

Matthew 5:11 forewarns, *"Blessed are ye, when men shall revile you, and persecute you, and shall say all manner of evil against you falsely, for my sake."* Interestingly, we do not count it as a blessing when someone mistreats us. Similarly, Matthew 11:6 advises, *"And blessed is he, whosoever shall not be offended in me."*

Church hurt is supposed, prolonged, hostility, unkindness, ill-treatment, annoyance, or intimidation suffered by an inexperienced or immature believer at the hand of other believers. Most Church hurt comes from not knowing the Word of God. Experiencing Church hurt can break a person's heart and drive them far away from the Lord and the Church. If a person regularly experiences an unchecked Church hurt, they may also reach a point where they think about or carry out a plan to do physical harm to someone, including themselves.

Church hurt does not have to be intentional or real; it can be accidental and imagined. Undoubtedly, if the recipient believes someone in the Church is persecuting them, they will experience the effects of Church hurt. The signs of Church hurt include extreme sadness, tormenting thoughts, and mental anguish, which attacks a person's self-esteem. These thoughts often tell the individual they are

27

worthless, and no one cares about them, including the Lord Jesus. They will often feel alienated and ashamed and may also struggle with a desire for vengeance. Loneliness is one of the chief experiences of someone encountering Church hurt, as they may not have anyone who understands their situation. Furthermore, the trauma individuals undergo due to Church hurt consists of running from Church to Church in search of a suitable Church environment, only to find the same confusion everywhere they go.

Immature believers find it difficult to see the love of God in Church hurt. They do not understand how they can benefit from others hurting them. Because they have preconceived ideas about Christianity, they do not comprehend how Church folk can hurt one another willfully or unintentionally. However, sometimes believers hurt one another because they are: unwise, experiencing Church hurt, insensitive, or are unknowingly being used by the Lord to bring about growth in the one experiencing the hurt.

For example, when I first gave my life to Jesus, the Holy Spirit actively worked to transform my worldly behavior to Christ-like behavior. So, to test my character, the Lord allowed an incident to happen with someone in the choir. It was during a rehearsal for an upcoming concert. We were sitting in the pews, and suddenly, without warning, a choir member purposefully and forcefully jabbed me with her elbow. It was unprovoked, and I was nearly in a rage. Then she began to say, "What are you going to do, Fern!" She continued to ramble many unintelligent words and threats. I knew it was the Lord, yet I was angry.

I initially thought, girl, you just hit the wrong person, but instead of knocking her block off, I looked around the sanctuary. I started counting up the cost of a violent reaction. I wondered what would happen to my testimony. I began to speak within myself, "If you do not let this go, you will always be considered the crazy girl who was fighting in the Church." I also thought, "The Lord will not be able to use me because I will stay bound by the adversary and my flesh if I don't pass this test." So, I quickly decided to ignore her and let it go. Then she said, "I thought so. You ain't gone do nothing."

I never told anyone what happened. I am so thankful I let it go because I realized I was on the road to being delivered from a worldly spirit, and she was used to test me. Afterward, I frequently saw that sister at Church, and I did not hold the incident against her. Again, I let it go and saw it for what it was, the Lord testing my character. It's funny because she conducted herself like nothing ever happened. I mean, she was walking around like she had no remembrance of it happening.

I have experienced Church hurt several times, and each time my heart ripped differently than it did in the previous experience. Before my heart could heal from one injury, another injury emerged. The type of injury specifically determined the measure of pain and forgiveness necessary to get through the situation. Although the events were getting more serious, the Lord was targeting a specific area of my character which needed correction. He was also addressing my mindset.

Before I gave my life to Jesus, I was slow to forgive and would quickly sever relationships with those who had hurt me. So, when people in the Church wounded me, the Lord specifically told me I had to forgive and love as if nothing had happened. And I had to forgive quickly. The most significant part of the pain was submitting to mistreatment and not defending myself. During those seasons, I cried a lot because I could not run, retaliate, or complain. I had to hold my peace and pray. You see, unconditional love will not keep a record of wrong. It will not retaliate, and it will not run and tell others what is going on.

The measure of love I possess has grown over the years by cooperating with the Holy Ghost. The degree of the Holy Spirit that dwells within a person determines the amount of love a person possesses. The ability to forgive is measured by how much a person allows the Holy Spirit of God to lead them. When they crucified Jesus, He did not retaliate. He said in Luke 23:34, *". . . Father, forgive them; for they know not what they do."* I needed to get to a place where I forgave those who hurt me, so my pain would heal.

When I was going through one particular instance of Church hurt, I noticed I wept all the time. All I could do was pray because I felt so beat down. As I prayed, the peace of God would overwhelm me, and I felt strengthened to go on another day. However, afterward, something reminded me of my pain, and the tears came again. Many around me were selfish; they only thought of themselves. They did not discern my anxiety, and if they did, they did not care. Some added to my pain by mishandling me, thinking they were doing the will of God. I heard some of them say, "Oh! It will make her stronger. Strengthen her, Lord!" I heard others rejoice at my pain. I was often confused. One day they loved me, and the next, they injured me all over again.

Those around me misunderstood my intentions. They thought I was against them. They did not know me as I genuinely am, although they thought they did. During that time, I was regularly in others' presence, so I hid my face because the tears were sometimes spontaneous. Many times, I could not stop crying. Then the crying started to get so bad I did not care who saw me because it became impossible to stop the tears' continuous flow. I desired to tell others what was going on with me. Maybe they would then see the error of their ways and comfort me. I preferred to scream. Perhaps someone would pity me, but that would only have taken away from the beauty of the test. It would nullify all the Lord was trying to do in me.

If I opened my mouth, it might have uttered things it must not. Where was my place of refuge? My refuge certainly was not in the bosom of man. My only place of refuge was in the presence of the Lord. I could not walk, run, or drive away from fellowship with Him because the Comforter is present within me. The Holy Spirit is my Comforter. He is my hiding place. When His peace overwhelmed me, my spirit would become quiet again, and I felt no need to share my pain with others.

The Book of Psalms 91:1-16 declares, *"HE that dwelleth in the secret place of the most High shall abide under the shadow of the*

32

Almighty. I will say of the LORD, He is my refuge and my fortress: my God; in him will I trust. Surely he shall deliver thee from the snare of the fowler, and from the noisome pestilence. He shall cover thee with his feathers, and under his wings shalt thou trust: his truth shall be thy shield and buckler. Thou shalt not be afraid for the terror by night; nor for the arrow that flieth by day; Nor for the pestilence that walketh in darkness; nor for the destruction that wasteth at noonday. A thousand shall fall at thy side, and ten thousand at thy right hand; but it shall not come nigh thee. Only with thine eyes shalt thou behold and see the reward of the wicked. Because thou hast made the LORD, which is my refuge, even the most High, thy habitation; There shall no evil befall thee, neither shall any plague come nigh thy dwelling. For he shall give his angels charge over thee, to keep thee in all thy ways. They shall bear thee up in their hands, lest thou dash thy foot against a stone. Thou shalt tread upon the lion and adder: the young lion and the dragon shalt thou trample under feet. Because he hath set his love upon me, therefore will I deliver him: I will set him on high, because he hath known my name. He shall call upon me, and I will answer him: I will be with him in trouble; I will deliver him, and honour him. With long life will I satisfy him, and shew him my salvation."

I knew the Lord was in control. As long as I allowed Him to be Lord in my life, I was at peace. I am reminded of the Scriptures in Isaiah 64:1-9. The Lord extends His arm of love to us while we are going through seasons of hurt. It is in times of adversity that our faith is tested and tried. In our brokenness, we see the error of our ways. Only then do we begin to earnestly seek the Lord without pretense, perpetration, or falsehood. When we are miserable, the things we do and say are authentic. In times of affliction, we come to know the real reason we are serving the Lord. Is it just for blessings? It is only through hardship that we come to realize whether we sincerely desire to do the Lord's will instead of our own.

The bottom line is we all will go through difficult and unpleasant seasons in our walk with the Lord. However, we must use those seasons to get into the Lord's presence like we never have before. That is the time for our souls to seek after and thirst for Him. The Lord should not always have to pursue us to draw us into His presence. When we come to know who He is, we will seek Him. He will be our delight. Psalm 42:1-11 consoles my heart, *"AS the hart panteth after the water brooks, so panteth my soul after thee, O God. My soul thirsteth for God, for the living God: when shall I come and appear before God? My tears have been my meat day and night,*

34

while they continually say unto me, Where is thy God? When I remember these things, I pour out my soul in me: for I had gone with the multitude, I went with them to the house of God, with the voice of joy and praise, with a multitude that kept holyday. Why art thou cast down, O my soul? and why art thou disquieted in me? hope thou in God: for I shall yet praise him for the help of his countenance. O my God, my soul is cast down within me: therefore will I remember thee from the land of Jordan (my descend or flow down), and of the Hermonites (sacred mountain), from the hill Mizar (little). Deep calleth unto deep at the noise of thy waterspouts: all thy waves and thy billows are gone over me. Yet the LORD will command his lovingkindness in the daytime, and in the night his song shall be with me, and my prayer unto the God of my life. I will say unto God my rock, Why hast thou forgotten me? why go I mourning because of the oppression of the enemy? As with a sword in my bones, mine enemies reproach me; while they say daily unto me, Where is thy God? Why art thou cast down, O my soul? and why art thou disquieted within me? hope thou in God: for I shall yet praise him, who is the health of my countenance, and my God."

During the darkest hours, you will question whether you are hearing from the Lord. The Holy Ghost will be encouraging you on one side, and those in the Church who hear the Lord's voice will often unknowingly deliver discouraging unsupportive words on the other side. These words may appear to be the opposite of what the Holy Ghost spoke to you. However, if you listen carefully, you will hear the same voice, no matter the vessel. So, whom should you listen to when it comes to hearing from the Lord? Should you listen to the Lord in everyone else, or do you believe what the Lord is saying to you directly?

Throughout seasons of Church hurt, you are in a scary place spiritually. Make sure you do not shut down communication with the Lord, whether directly or indirectly. I have found contradictions are from the Lord. It most likely means the enemy is fighting to nullify the Lord's plan for your life. One meaning has to do with what will happen to you if you decide to leave the Lord and not serve Him. And the other has to do with your decision to continue to endure your tests and do the will of God. In these situations, stand still and do not make any decisions one way or the other. Wait on the Lord to reveal the truth. The only thing you should be doing is spending time in the Lord's presence. That will drive away confusion, and you will have peace. Cast your cares upon the Lord and wield the Word of God so you will not give up. If you forget anything the Lord said to you, encouraging and discouraging, good and bad, you will fail. Galatians 6:9 warns of this, *"And let us not be weary in well doing: for in due season we shall reap, if we faint not."*

The thing to remember about faith is if you lack faith in one area of your life, it will spread to all other parts of your existence. For example, let's say the Lord promised you something, and you wholeheartedly believe you will receive it. Then, years later, you get a word, which seems contrary, so you begin to doubt the original word. If you believe the contradictory statement, it will cause you to question everything else the Lord said or will say in the future. Faith in His promises must continue to the grave to ensure doubt does not spread to all areas of your walk.

The Lord must test your faith again and again. How many times have we said we have faith in the Lord, and then we start going through a situation and immediately begin to question the Lord's plan? Is that faith? No, it is not. Rightfully, the brethren are faithful in allowing the Lord to unknowingly use them to challenge our faith to see if we truly believe. James 1:2-4 declares, *"My brethren, count it all joy when ye fall into divers temptations; Knowing this, that the trying of your faith worketh patience. But let patience have her perfect work, that ye may be perfect and entire, wanting nothing."* Remember, our faith will always be a work in progress.

I reiterate, when you are in a season of brokenness, the best thing to do is spend a lot of time with the Lord, be silent, standstill, and do not leave the Church (unless the Lord is telling you to go). Let the Lord have His way with you. Follow the leading and guidance of the Holy Spirit. If you let the Lord work in you, you will soon realize things were not as bad as you thought, and some whom you believed to oppose you were praying for you and your well-being.

Most of the time, when people in the Church hurt you, they sincerely believe they are doing what is best for you. Although they may be handling the situation poorly or are just wrong in their view of you, they have good intentions. The truth is when the Lord is working on you, reshaping and remolding your character, no one will know what is going on with you. He desires your brokenness, only depending on Him. The Word of God encourages us in 1st Peter 5:6-7 to *"Humble yourselves therefore under the mighty hand of God, that he may exalt you in due time: Casting all your care upon him; for he careth for you."*

Reader, pray this prayer with me:

Abba, Father, in the name of Jesus Christ of Nazareth, reveal to me the beauty of my test and trial. I do not see my situation the way I should. Show me how You see my life and renew my mind in every area displeasing to You. I know there is a reason I'm going through this particular trial. If it was something I did or said, show me. If You are addressing a mindset, please show me. Allow me to see things how You see them. Show me what You are addressing by this trial. Help me to see Your hand in everything I'm going through. Grant me to know Your thoughts and ways. I fully cooperate and commit myself to the power of the Holy Ghost in this process. I will not resist or run. I will fall upon the rock, Jesus Christ, my Lord. In the name of Jesus, Amen!

CHAPTER THREE

THE TRYING OF YOUR FAITH

*". . . but we glory in tribulations also: knowing that
tribulation worketh patience;"*

Romans 5:3 (b-c only)

CHAPTER 3: *THE TRYING OF YOUR FAITH*

The Book of James 1:2-4 declares, *"My brethren, count it all joy when ye fall into divers temptations; Knowing this, that the trying of your faith worketh patience. But let patience have her perfect work, that ye may be perfect and entire, wanting nothing."* There is a time for the Lord to try our faith. It is inescapable. The growth and development of our character depend on the proving of our faith. To go deeper in our relationship with the Lord, we must allow Him to correct our character. However, most do not welcome the hardships that are necessary for our character to grow and change. Instead, an unusual number of believers seek to alleviate suffering.

The question is when it's time for you to mature: How will you go through your test? Who will you blame for your test? Will you blame God? Will you blame the saints, the brethren? Will you blame the Church leaders? Will you blame some Christian you know somewhere who was not an example to you? Will you blame your spouse or your children? When believers go through tests or trials, they look at everyone except themselves. Saints rarely consider it was immaturity or a wrong mindset on our part that brought on the test or trial. Notwithstanding, some things are just the will of God. Again, we all have to suffer if we hope to reign with Christ (2nd Timothy 2:12).

We also encounter tests when something in our character displeases the Lord, which we do not desire to face. Although we shy away from dealing with our shortcomings, tests are the Lord's way of expelling our flaws to the surface so we can deal with them. Think about it like this; our faults are like the fault lines in the Earth; if they are not corrected, they will eventually cause disturbances. To my understanding, only Jesus can correct a fault, so when He grants an opportunity to correct an area of our character, we must cooperate with Him, lest those hidden things continue to tear up our lives.

How do we know there is a fault in our character? Shortcomings are exposed when we do not respond to situations according to the Word of God. James 5:16 declares, *"Confess your faults one to another, and pray one for another, that ye may be healed. The effectual fervent prayer of a righteous man availeth much."* According to that passage of Scripture, faults are a sideslip, lapse, deviation, unintentional error, willful transgression, fall, offense, sin, or trespass (S.C. 3900 Gk.). We must confess our faults to release our healing. The problem is we have to pray for one another for our healing to take place. I'm saying it is a problem because most people do not spend time in prayer. Wow! We have to pray to receive our healing when others hurt us. Yes, pray and do not gossip. Pray and do not retaliate. When you gossip instead of praying, you use your words to throw punches at the person you are slandering. Gossip is how you defend yourself. Gossip is how you hurt the reputation of the other person. But, it will destroy you spiritually and naturally. The Lord hates those who sow discord amongst the brethren. *"These six things doth the LORD hate: . . . A false witness that speaketh lies, and he that soweth discord among brethren"* (Proverbs 6:16 and 19).

Unforgivingness and lovelessness are two of the most significant faults operating in the Body of Christ. Many can attest to someone in the Church who hurt their feelings or did them wrong in one way or another. Reader, you may not know it, but you have also hurt, offended, harmed (done damage to someone's spiritual health), or done someone wrong in the Church. It is never about other people; it is always about us. If we keep running when situations happen or ignore the Lord's unctions to examine and renew that area of our character, we will likely enter a test. Depending on how long we have been running, we may enter test after test. Instead of praying everyone involved receives healing, we often complain, fight back (railing for railing), or involve someone else in the situation, all leading to unforgivingness.

Forgiveness and healing go together. When we do not forgive, a series of things happen: the Lord does not forgive us, and we do not receive our healing. Furthermore, unforgivingness causes us to hold the matter over the offender's head as if we are putting them in prison. Frequently, the other person feels the resentment emitted, and they begin to change how they see the Church. And sometimes, they turn against God. Some feel seriously injured and retaliate against the offender, causing stagnation for the injured party. By not forgiving the offender, we prevent them from seeing and experiencing the love of God through us. Hebrews 12:14-15 declares, *"Follow peace with all men, and holiness, without which no man shall see the Lord: Looking diligently lest any man fail of the grace of God; lest any root of bitterness springing up trouble you, and thereby many be defiled;"*

Think about unforgivingness and the root of bitterness. Not only does unforgivingness and bitterness damage the offender, but it also hurts the one offended. The offender gets hurt when the one offended has a retaliatory mindset, although the offender has forgotten the incident. People who are easily offended are often those who take everything personally. Unforgivingness not only seeks to imprison the offender; the one who refuses to forgive is brought into bondage as well because they lose the power to move forward. They also lose many blessings and suffer the loss of all manner of relationships. Ultimately, their relationship with the Lord suffers. When we refuse to forgive, we force the Lord into a position of being unable to forgive us for our trespasses and offenses, at which point we remain broken. The Book of Mark 11:26 declares, *"But if ye do not forgive, neither will your Father which is in heaven forgive your trespasses."*

Sometimes the offender is an immature saint who lacks understanding, and a seemingly mature saint is offended. Believers who have been around the Church a long time tend to hold immature saints to the same standard the Lord holds them to, which is very displeasing to the Lord. Many Churches are not bearing fruit, and God's power cannot flow because of the lack of forgiveness and love in the Church. Too many saints are bitter and angry because of something someone said or did to them, and for years they will not let it go.

The root of bitterness and unforgivingness are intertwined. Unforgivingness causes a root of bitterness, and a source of bitterness strengthens unforgivingness to the point where the one offended struggles to forgive. Forgiveness heals us spiritually and naturally, and unforgivingness causes sickness and disease spiritually and naturally. Unforgivingness changes your outlook on life from a positive outlook to a negative outlook. Furthermore, it will change how you see the Lord. Job's wife said in Job 2:9, *"... Dost thou still retain thine integrity? curse God, and die."* Her outlook changed because of her mourning. She was growing bitter because the fruit of her womb perished. *"But he said unto her, Thou speakest as one of the foolish women speaketh. What? shall we receive good at the hand of God, and shall we not receive evil? In all this did not Job sin with his lips"* (Job 2:10).

Not only do those offended hold on to the offense, but they also involve as many people as possible who will listen. Gossip is a sign a person has a root of bitterness, which defiles many in the Church. Why do we feel the need to involve others in our test? Their involvement just intensifies it and causes the Lord to lengthen the process. The problem with involving others is if you see the error of your ways and repent, it is often impossible to go to all those you polluted and get it right with them. And if you have an issue with pride, then you really will not go to those you corrupted and tell them

48

you were wrong. You will not tell them the test was about you and not the offender.

How will any of us know the power of forgiveness if people do not hurt us? How will we know how deep our love goes if people do not injure us? When others hurt us, we feel all manner of emotions and experience all forms of reactions. And when the Lord is working amid a trial, we experience the hurt and pain even deeper than we would under normal circumstances because the Word of God limits our response. Ideally, we are limited by our requirement to respond maturely as believers who strive to please the Lord. The purpose is to draw repentance, forgiveness, and love out of the depths of our character. To truly forgive, we must experience something we would not usually forgive with ease. The Word of God declares in Romans 5:8, *"But God commendeth his love toward us, in that, while we were yet sinners, Christ died for us."* People do not have to deserve our love or forgiveness. We are required to extend it freely, so we will experience the love of God and forgiveness when we sin against the Lord. We also freely forgive so the offender can see the error of their ways and likewise experience the love and mercy of God.

The Bible declares in Ecclesiastes 7:9, *"Be not hasty in thy spirit to be angry: for anger resteth in the bosom of fools."* The Word of God declares anger resteth; that is, it continually takes a seat in one's bosom. It becomes a part of who you are. Only a foolish person will hold on to something that will make them physically and spiritually sick, tired, and hateful. Anger is so toxic it causes headaches, digestive problems, sleep disorders, muscle tension, libido changes, high blood pressure, skin rashes, heart disease, depression, cancer, strokes, miscarriages, and more? Frankly, anger will shorten your days. It will kill you! I knew someone who dropped dead while in a rage.

When offenses linger, anger develops. It happens in an instant. Yet, in an instant, we have the choice to be angry or forgiving. When you choose anger instead of forgiveness and peace, anger drains your vitality and strength and releases poisons in your body. That is why many feel extremely tired or sick after bouts of anger. The Book of Ephesians 4:26-27 declares, *"Be ye angry, and sin not: let not the sun go down upon your wrath: Neither give place to the devil."* Anger is a natural part of human nature, yet it can cause you to lose yourself in ways you can't imagine. It can open a door for the devil to come in and wreak havoc in your entire life. Once a person starts on the path of anger, it is difficult to get them off that path. A person operating in anger is unreasonably unjust and blind.

First, an evil spirit will trouble the angry person and plague their mind with all manner of evil thoughts about the offender and the trespass. These thoughts trouble the individual until they decide to take action and do damage to the offender. Second, the plotting begins. An angry person will not be satisfied, and their anger will not cease until the offender is injured. An angry person will not rest until the deed done is recompensed, no matter how small the offense. Third, unforgivingness and hatred begin to drive the individual. No matter what the offender does to try and make the situation right, the offender will not be successful in turning the heart of the one they offended back to Christ. I say, turning them back to Christ because anyone operating in anger has unforgivingness and is in a place in the Lord that needs serious consideration. Their sins remain as long as they refuse to forgive. James 5:19-20 informs us, *"Brethren, if any of you do err from the truth, and one convert him; Let him know, that he which converteth the sinner from the error of his way shall save a soul from death, and shall hide a multitude of sins."*

The Bible gives clear instructions on how to handle these situations, yet it is up to us to accept the Word of God and choose to walk therein. Matthew 5:22-24 declares, *"But I say unto you, That whosoever is angry with his brother without a cause shall be in danger of the judgment: and whosoever shall say to his brother, Raca, shall be in danger of the council: but whosoever shall say, Thou fool, shall be in danger of hell fire. Therefore if thou bring thy gift to the altar, and there rememberest that thy brother hath ought against thee; Leave there thy gift before the altar, and go thy way; first be reconciled to thy brother, and then come and offer thy gift."*

The Bible instructs us to reconcile our relationship with our brother. It is more important than giving gifts and offerings to the Lord. Sometimes reconciliation is a long process, yet you have to start somewhere. Matthew 18:15-17 declares, *"Moreover if thy brother shall trespass against thee, go and tell him his fault between thee and him alone: if he shall hear thee, thou hast gained thy brother. But if he will not hear thee, then take with thee one or two more, that in the mouth of two or three witnesses every word may be established. And if he shall neglect to hear them, tell it unto the church: but if he neglect to hear the church, let him be unto thee as an heathen man and a publican."* That passage of Scripture declares unity is so crucial to our success in the Lord that the person who breaks the bond of unity by refusing to forgive and restore harmony is to receive the same treatment one would give an uncivilized person.

According to Easton's Bible Dictionary, a publican outsourced to subordinates the responsibility to collect government taxes from a town or district (e.g., Zacchaeus in Luke 19:2). The subordinates often extorted and embezzled more than was due. Taxes were then paid to the Romans and were considered grievous to the Jews. Furthermore, many of the tax collectors were Jews who were subsequently shunned and hated for their role in the matter. So being compared to a publican is shameful. It is a shame when we, as believers, wallow in anger and unforgivingness.

Colossians 3:8-10 declares, *"But now ye also put off all these; anger, wrath, malice, blasphemy, filthy communication out of your mouth. Lie not one to another, seeing that ye have put off the old man with his deeds; And have put on the new man, which is renewed in knowledge after the image of him that created him:"* When we are hurting it is not easy to put off anger. However, we must strive to do so to please the Lord. If nothing else, we have to realize it is never about the other person. It is about us as individuals staying in a mindset of fearing the Lord. James 1:20 declares, *"For the wrath of man worketh not the righteousness of God."*

The best thing to do during the season of resisting anger is to spend as much time as possible with the Lord. Lie before Him in prayer and worship, and read the Word of God. And, it is not about studying a group of Scriptures on anger. Let the Lord lead you concerning the Scriptures to research so you can discover some things about yourself during that season. You may find you have a habit of getting angry when someone commits a specific offense against you. The Lord may be allowing you to experience repeated wrongdoings to show you something about yourself. We won't know what is in us until we experience something that will shake that area of our life. And once you come to terms with the truth that the LORD is in control, you will be less apt to be angry with others. Remember, letting go of anger may take some time as you heal from the many wounds you have received in life and the Church.

Reader, pray this prayer with me:

Abba, Father, in the name of Jesus Christ of Nazareth, teach me to know Thy ways. Give me a delight in serving You. Search my heart and reveal to me all those things displeasing to You. Reveal to me what is causing me to be angry, whether it be generational or something present in my life. I command anger to come out of my bosom. I ask that the peace of God will rest in my bosom. Grant me understanding to know how to please You in the different situations I face daily, in the name of Jesus Christ of Nazareth.

CHAPTER FOUR

CHURCH IS A PROVING GROUND

"And he that taketh not his cross, and followeth after me, is not worthy of me."

Matthew 10:38

CHAPTER 4: *CHURCH IS A PROVING GROUND*

The Lord never promised a daisy walk in Him where we only experience affectionate love in the Church. With a daisy walk, everyone is understanding, encouraging, kind, and unselfish. Unfortunately, serving the Lord is more like walking through a rose garden, sweet-smelling and thorny, with lots of bees during the time of pollination. When disturbed, bees can be an annoyance and are sometimes dangerous, even deadly.

In our walk with the Lord, we will find seasons of all manner of challenges in life, some pleasant and some unpleasant. We will also encounter all kinds of people, some with our best interest at heart and some who will be narcissistic. We will meet people who will try to make our lives miserable. However, if we can roll with the punches, we will likely find love lessons in everything we experience in our walk with the Lord.

The Lord has a way of not interfering when we begin to experience things in life. He allows life to run its course because whatever we are going through is part of His grand plan for us to develop the Holy Ghost's virtues. Galatians 5:22-25 declares, *"But the fruit of the Spirit is love, joy, peace, longsuffering, gentleness, goodness, faith, Meekness, temperance: against such there is no law. And they that are Christ's have crucified the flesh with the affections and lusts. If we live in the Spirit, let us also walk in the Spirit."* Which virtues of the Holy Ghost do you possess? If you believe you have some elements of the fruit of the Spirit, great! However, the problem is what you lack. The missing parts keep you from living the Word of God. That is the area of your character the Lord is addressing, but He needs your cooperation to complete the work. If you refuse to work together with the Holy Ghost, you will find yourself getting more frustrated. Frustration is a sign you are not in agreement with the Lord in some area of your life. That is when you need to examine whether you are bearing fruit. At that point, the perfect question to ask is which virtues do I lack?

Let's see. Have you ever hurt so much it felt like your heart was bleeding? That was a time when the Lord did not answer your cries for help; neither did He intervene to lessen or stop your pain. It was during that time that you thought you could not hurt any deeper. Well, that shows you lacked the virtue of longsuffering. The blessing in staying in a season of pain is it draws you closer to the Lord as He renews you in every area: mind, spirit, and character. Longsuffering brings about renewal. If you stay in the season without complaining

60

and gossiping, you will find humility and the fruit of the Spirit growing inside of you. Also, the Lord will increase your understanding as you read the Word of God. You will no longer see those who hurt you as enemies but as souls who need prayer.

When you pray for someone who has hurt you to prosper and receive strength in the Lord, it is the virtue of love in operation. Yet if you pray witchcraft prayers over those who have hurt you, then the attributes of the Holy Ghost cease to come forth. I remember a time in the Church when I was praying for a young lady who was regularly doing evil toward me. I always prayed for her strength, yet she wished evil upon me. I know it happened because she confessed to me that she was sending spirits to attack me regularly. Even though I knew what she was doing, I continued to pray she would gain strength and move forward in the Lord. Sadly, she never prospered and eventually left the Lord. Yet, I gained strength to love with a greater level of compassion, which I needed later when I encountered another test. The Lord will also increase your anointing and empower you to move forward and prosper in Him if you go through the trial without defiling others with your situation. The question is can you pass the test? The proving ground validates your level of maturity, faith, and love. It demonstrates to the world the virtues you possess.

Furthermore, the Lord never promised there would not be people hurting one another. However, He did instruct what to do when injuries happen in life. In my experience, when you go to someone who has hurt you, most of the time, they will receive you. However, if on the rare occasion you are not accepted, forgive anyway and let it go. Letting it go also brings about healing and the ability to forgive more quickly the next time someone hurts you, and there will be a next time. The way you grow in love is to respond in love to the opportunities the Lord sends your way. If someone comes to you and says you offended or hurt them agree with them quickly to settle the matter and restore peace amongst the brethren because that is how the virtue of peace will be birthed in you and will be shed abroad to others. Remember, it is all a test.

I remembered many years ago, a sister in the Church called me at home and said she needed to speak with me about something important. I could hear the urgency in her voice and knew she felt uneasy discussing it with me. I immediately went to a private place in the house. She began to explain how I hurt her two weeks earlier while on our way to Church. She said she prayed for two weeks on the situation. She desired the Lord to prepare me to receive her and what she had to say. She asked me if I remembered what I had told

62

her. I replied, "Yes." I immediately remembered callously saying something along the lines of I do not desire to be around someone who does not have faith. She explained it was not that she lacked faith, but she was in a faith test and was doing everything to hold on to the measure of faith the Lord had given her. There was no need for me to explain since what I said to her was not the issue at hand. The bottom line was I needed to acknowledge I hurt her feelings and repent so she could have peace. Why would I deny her the peace she needed?

Once she finished talking, I immediately began to repent to her and ask for her forgiveness. I did not defend myself, nor did I make excuses. She was shocked the phone call was so easy. It was a big test to see how we would handle the situation and was our opportunity to operate in genuine love and forgiveness. It was also an opportunity to glorify the Lord. There was no arguing or debating, only repentance, love, and forgiveness. We also felt great joy and excitement after having received each other. There will be no blessing upon our offerings if we are sitting in Church offended. The Lord does not receive our worship or gifts unless they are with a sincere and forgiving heart. A sincere heart will seek peace and forgive the brethren.

To be honest, I forgot about my statement to her. Insensitivity followed me for years until the Lord began to break my heart so I could relate to others. It did not feel good when I went through heartbreak tests, yet it all worked out for my good with time. I can honestly say I am grateful the Lord did and is still doing the work in me.

The Word of God commands us to mortify the deeds of the flesh. Without tests, we will never know if we have mortified our earthly nature. If the Lord does not test us, we will never see the realness of being a new creature in Christ. The Scriptures declare, *"Mortify therefore your members which are upon the earth; fornication, uncleanness, inordinate affection, evil concupiscence, and covetousness, which is idolatry: For which things' sake the wrath of God cometh on the children of disobedience: In the which ye also walked some time, when ye lived in them. But now ye also put off all these; anger, wrath, malice, blasphemy, filthy communication out of your mouth. Lie not one to another, seeing that ye have put off the old man with his deeds; And have put on the new man, which is renewed in knowledge after the image of him that created him:"* (Colossians 3:5-10).

Over and over, the Bible instructs us to crucify the flesh and not fulfill its lusts (Galatians 5:24 and 5:16). Again, without tests, how will you know you are free from the desires of the flesh? You will not know unless the Lord tailor makes a test or trial just for you. *"For the flesh lusteth against the Spirit, and the Spirit against the flesh: and these are contrary the one to the other: so that ye cannot do the things that ye would. But if ye be led of the Spirit, ye are not under the law"* (Galatians 5:17-18).

The Lord designed every test I have gone through. Each trial had the divine purpose of helping me see something about myself. Whether it was something I was operating in or a mindset, there was a purpose for the test. My assignment was to walk in the virtues of the Holy Spirit through my trial and pray earnestly. I also had to wait for the Lord to reveal the error of my ways and acknowledge that error. After repentance, then and only then did I find I had a renewed mind and heart (character). So, you will experience hurts and pains in the Church. Remember, the Church is the proving ground. If you do not desire to live in harmony with the saints on Earth, you do not plan to live in Heaven because it is full of saints! Hallelujah!

Reader, pray this prayer with me:

Abba, Father, in the name of Jesus Christ of Nazareth, help me stand amid injuries in the Church. Help me remain in the Church where You placed me when I feel like giving up. Lord Jesus, don't let me walk away from my inheritance. Lord, keep me in righteousness, in Jesus' name. Amen!

CHAPTER FIVE

WHY PERSECUTEST THOU ME?

"When my father and my mother forsake me, then the LORD will take me up."

Psalm 27:10

CHAPTER 5: *WHY PERSECUTEST THOU ME?*

"AND Saul, yet breathing out threatenings and slaughter against the disciples of the Lord, went unto the high priest, And desired of him letters to Damascus to the synagogues, that if he found any of this way, whether they were men or women, he might bring them bound unto Jerusalem. And as he journeyed, he came near Damascus: and suddenly there shined round about him a light from heaven: And he fell to the earth, and heard a voice saying unto him, Saul, Saul, why persecutest thou me? And he said, Who art thou, Lord? And the Lord said, I am Jesus whom thou persecutest: it is hard for thee to kick against the pricks" (Acts 9:1-5). To kick against the pricks is to kick your bare feet against a thorn. It is the unfortunate result of resisting the will of God.

Notice in that passage of Scripture, the high priest gave Saul his request for letters addressed to the synagogues in Damascus. The high priest was supposed to be God's representative. However, the high priests had no understanding of what the Lord was doing in the Earth at that time. The Lord hardened their hearts and did not allow them to perceive the Messiah. It is the same way today; the saints are the ones persecuting the Church. Oh! We don't do it with letters threatening to bind and imprison those who believe in and preach Jesus. But, we persecute the Lord by stopping saints from leaving a Church to fulfill the Lord's vision. We persecute by attempting to silence those who carry the Word of the Lord.

Many saints also persecute Jesus by leaving a ministry and telling everything they think they know about the Church to make the leaders and the brethren bear the guilt for their departure from the Lord. The intent is to remove their responsibility for things they did or did not do while attending a particular ministry. It's like a child running away from home. When asked why they left, they refused to say, "I was rebellious and did not desire to obey my parents." Instead, they say, "My parents wronged me. They never understood me. They favored my brother. They loved my sister more. They never listened to me. They were horrible!" Accusations against the Church attempt to divert others from serving the Lord by ruining the Church's credibility. It is an attempt to hurt the leaders.

It is impossible to find a perfect Church because ministries are full of humans who are sick. For that reason, every Church has the potential to be a target of gossip. Spiritual leaders cannot please everyone; neither should they try. They should only seek to please the Lord. Jesus said in Matthew 9:12 c-only and 9:13, ". . . *They that be whole need not a physician, but they that are sick. But go ye and learn what that meaneth, I will have mercy, and not sacrifice: for I am not come to call the righteous, but sinners to repentance."*

Most of the time, believers complain continuously about the brethren or their leaders. They claim someone is always stepping on their toes, but instead of staying and showing everyone how to be a "good saint," they leave complaining. They don't pray because they are too busy complaining. People who spend a lot of time in prayer do not have time to complain or gossip. Moreover, some believers abandon ministries and spread lies to cripple the Church even more. They also keep in contact with those still attending the ministry to draw them away from the Lord. That tactic gives the backslider a good excuse for leaving. Then those in the world say to them, "If all that was going on in that Church, I don't blame you for leaving." All the talking and complaining brings shame and reproach on the Body of Christ, and sometimes it is so extensive a ministry cannot recover. It also hinders souls from being saved, and that alone displeases the Lord.

When backsliders leave a Church running their mouths, the enemies of the Lord blaspheme. I do not desire to be the catalyst the enemy uses to damage a Church. Jesus, thou son of David, have

71

mercy on me! I need a touch from You, Jesus! *"And they which went before rebuked him, that he should hold his peace: but he cried so much the more, Thou son of David, have mercy on me"* (Luke 18:39). Those following the Lord were the ones telling the man in that Scripture to hold his peace. Some in the Church are hurting many souls because of religion. Christians are persecuting the Church more than anyone else because they do not understand the Lord's ways. *"O the depth of the riches both of the wisdom and knowledge of God! how unsearchable are his judgments, and his ways past finding out"* Romans 11:33!

Most times, the Lord uses those in the Church to refine you. He draws on every situation necessary to help you get some character. Yet, if you leave bashing the Church, you will only hurt yourself, and you will continue to lack the measure of character needed to pass tests in the future. As a rule of thumb, the Lord is not pleased when we speak ill of anyone, and frankly, it is not wise because what you say about others will be the very thing the Lord will allow to come upon you if you do not correct your mindset and your ways. I am telling you what I know firsthand.

Romans 13:10-14 admonishes, *"Love worketh no ill to his neighbour: therefore love is the fulfilling of the law. And that,*

72

knowing the time, that now it is high time to awake out of sleep: for now is our salvation nearer than when we believed. The night is far spent, the day is at hand: let us therefore cast off the works of darkness, and let us put on the armour of light. Let us walk honestly, as in the day; not in rioting and drunkenness, not in chambering and wantonness, not in strife and envying. But put ye on the Lord Jesus Christ, and make not provision for the flesh, to fulfil the lusts thereof." All this I pray for the reader in the name of Jesus Christ of Nazareth.

Some time ago, I heard a musician who experienced Church hurt say, "When we leave a Church, we should tell everything that's going on. We need to expose these Churches for what they truly are." Please understand certain positions in life require integrity. If you cannot keep classified what you see and experience at a Church, you are untrustworthy and have no business in those positions. Evidence of your unfaithfulness is the counsel to others to "tell everything." The Bible declares in Proverbs 11:13, *"A talebearer revealeth secrets: be he that is of a faithful spirit concealeth the matter."* Frankly, advising people to tell everything sounds like a rash recommendation for several reasons.

Firstly, Romans 14:4 declares, *"Who art thou that judgest another man's servant? to his own master he standeth or falleth. Yea, he shall be holden up: for God is able to make him stand."* If the Church leaders are wrong, the Lord will judge them. If the brethren are in error, the Lord will judge them. If the Church basher is wrong, the Lord will judge them too. It is reckless to talk about saints because no one is perfect. Would you desire for all your sins or shortcomings to be known to the world? When someone says tell everything that is going on, they are saying to the Lord, let all my faults be made known. Let everything I have going on behind the scenes be made public. Let the true nature of my wicked heart be made public. Let the wickedness of my imaginations be revealed openly. Lord, expose everything! Oh! I can hear that musician saying, "That's not what I meant, Lord! I meant tell on everyone else, but keep my mess a secret."

I would like to say to everyone who feels the same way as that musician: You have also made mistakes. The Lord will see to it that you do. It is misguided and wrong to be judgmental and self-righteous. The Bible declares in Isaiah 64:6, *"But we are all as an unclean thing, and all our righteousnesses are as filthy rags; and we all do fade as a leaf; and our iniquities, like the wind, have taken us away."* If you still feel you have no sin, then the Blood of Jesus is not for you. You do not need a savior because you are not sick. Jesus came for the sick. Thank you, Jesus, for dying for me and for saving me!

However! We know you, too, have sinned because 1st John 1:8-10 declares, *"If we say that we have no sin, we deceive ourselves, and the truth is not in us. If we confess our sins, he is faithful and just to forgive us our sins, and to cleanse us from all unrighteousness. If we say that we have not sinned, we make him a liar, and his word is not in us."* And we know God is not a liar. So, if Jesus saved you from something, and He continually does, because in our walk with Him, He is continuously revealing things we need to clean up, stop telling on everyone else, forgive, and pray for the brethren.

1st Thessalonians 5:16-23 instructs, *"Rejoice evermore. Pray without ceasing. In every thing give thanks: for this is the will of God in Christ Jesus concerning you. Quench not the Spirit. Despise not prophesyings. Prove all things; hold fast that which is good. Abstain from all appearance of evil. And the very God of peace sanctify you wholly; and I pray God your whole spirit and soul and body be preserved blameless unto the coming of our Lord Jesus Christ."*

Secondly, what if you are the one who is in the wrong? There are many sides to a situation: the Lord, the leader, you, and the brethren. Things are not only as you see them. Your perspective is not the only viewpoint, and usually, your point of view does not line up with how the Lord sees things, which is the only perspective that matters. When we go through something, it is often difficult to see things from another person's perspective. We must consider how the Lord sees the situation. We must ask, "What does the Lord require of me?" It is so hard to look at ourselves and consider why the situation is happening in the first place.

Thirdly, the Lord is the only one who can determine what is right and wrong. I know nothing happens in the Church that prayer, fasting, love, and forgiveness cannot heal. Yet Christians leave and run to another Church or break fellowship with the saints altogether before the Lord answers prayer or manifests His love and purpose in the situation. Often, the Lord takes His time answering prayers because most saints only spend time with Him when they are in some form of trouble or need Him to give them something.

Most of the time, a crisis in the Church is the Lord turning up the fire on individuals to get them to stop playing with Him and to draw them into a deeper place in their walk with Him. Ephesians 6:12

declares, *"For we wrestle not against flesh and blood, but against principalities, against powers, against the rulers of the darkness of this world, against spiritual wickedness in high places."* Although we know the Scripture, we carry ourselves as if it is not valid. We fight with people all day, and the battle rages on because we are not fighting the source through prayer, fasting, and the Word of God.

Fourthly, many in the Church have become menpleasers, and when men are not impressed, the menpleaser becomes angry and looks for ways to retaliate. The problem with gossiping about a Church after you leave is no one knows if you are just retaliating. Colossians 3:23-25 declares, *"And whatsoever ye do, do it heartily, as to the Lord, and not unto men; Knowing that of the Lord ye shall receive the reward of the inheritance: for ye serve the Lord Christ. But he that doeth wrong shall receive for the wrong which he hath done: and there is no respect of persons."* When you were in that particular ministry, you were supposed to be doing all you did as unto the Lord and not unto men. Since things did not turn out the way you hoped, there is no need to be angry or bitter. There is no reason to bad-mouth people. The Lord will repay if someone did you wrong. He will repay in His time and in His way. Additionally, don't leave unless the Lord is telling you to go. Why should you abort your mission in the Lord because of a misunderstanding between the saints?

Fifthly, what consequences will you suffer by talking about the Lord's servants? They are still His anointed. Study King David and King Saul in 1st Samuel 24:6-10 and 1st Samuel 26:9. Those familiar with the story usually agree that King Saul was wrong, yet the Lord is always in control. However, on two occasions, King David considered taking matters into his own hands and retaliating against King Saul, who was also the Lord's anointed. It doesn't matter whether the Lord was still with King Saul. The Lord anointed him into the office of King, and the Lord was the only one who could physically remove him from office. Unfortunately, David had to wait to take office after being anointed to replace King Saul. And everyone knew King Saul was not peaceful about being replaced by a shepherd boy. As we know, he pursued David many times to take his life, even taking the lives of priests and those wearing the linen ephod in his pursuit (1st Samuel 22:18).

The Lord's leaders always have a special anointing following them, especially in an Apostolic or Prophetic office. I'm talking about a Prophetic office, not the gift of prophecy. When someone speaks against or comes out against the Lord's Apostles, Prophets,

Prophetesses, Evangelists, or Pastors, the offender immediately activates consequences. Consider Moses and Aaron in the Book of Numbers, chapters 12, 13, 14, 16, and 17. Repeatedly, the congregation came out against Moses and Aaron and complained about their leadership. Unfortunately, the Lord responded with plagues, fires, natural disasters, stagnations, diseases, and deaths.

Furthermore, look at what 2nd Kings 2:23-24 declares about the Prophet Elisha, *"And he went up from thence unto Bethel: and as he was going up by the way, there came forth little children out of the city, and mocked him, and said unto him, Go up, thou bald head; go up, thou bald head. And he turned back, and looked on them, and cursed them in the name of the LORD. And there came forth two she bears out of the wood, and tare forty and two children of them."* Mocking a Prophet is a serious matter. It can cause lifelong hardships, and the person may not realize the difficulties stem from mistreating the Lord's servant. If the children in that passage of Scripture knew their lives were in danger for mocking a Prophet, would things have been different? Would they have been more respectful concerning the Man of God? I believe they would have exhibited proper reverence. I know too many examples where people came out against the Lord's servants and lost their lives.

79

There are many ways someone can come out against the Lord's anointed. Gossip is a primary weapon the adversary uses to fight against leaders. Unfortunately, today, some experience violence, like the Apostles, Prophets, and Priests did in the Bible. Moreover, some Church members do things to hinder the Lord's vision for a ministry. It is not uncommon for a Church to experience witchcraft attacks to halt the ministry's mission. Depending on the leader's anointing, the consequences for the one coming out against them could be poverty, loss of businesses, loss of homes and shelter, loss of livelihood, financial struggles, divorce, failure in school, calamities, loss of one's natural life, diseases, mental illness, a barren womb, loss of children, loss of natural beauty, starvation, imprisonment, missed callings, hardships and even loss of eternal life.

The Lord told me: *"When someone deliberately attempts to persecute a Church or a believer, they make themselves my direct enemy and an enemy of the Cross. The Church is not their enemy because I commanded the Church to love, pray, and forgive. That is the reason I had to deal with Saul of Tarsus directly. The early Church could not deal with him. I had to deal with him, and although I forgave him, he suffered greatly"* (2nd Corinthians 11:23-28). The early believers could not correct or persuade Saul to turn from his way, and they could not retaliate or defend themselves. They had to continue to spread the Gospel message. It is the same way today. So, the Lord repays in due time (Romans 12:19). Do you know once the Lord dealt with Saul of Tarsus, the Church had peace, but Paul suffered persecution? When you are the Lord's enemy, He will cause you to suffer, and He will give the people you are persecuting peace. Frankly, He will hurt you and mend them. If you repent, you may obtain mercy. However, if you do not repent, it will not go well for you.

In these cases, the offender must acknowledge God's sovereignty and repent, just as Saul of Tarsus had to repent in the Book of Acts 9:1-31. In all his zeal, Saul did not know that by persecuting Jesus' disciples, he was persecuting God. Once he was made aware of his error, there was no other option except to repent, and Saul was not concerned about what others thought of him. However, after his conversion, he began to suffer all manner of persecution, including stoning. What Paul did to the Church was recompensed unto him. He endured it without complaining because he understood it was by the Lord's hand.

Additionally, if you can, go to the person you persecuted and repent to them. Seek and beg the Lord earnestly for forgiveness. The reason I said beg is because these cases are more severe than saints believe. Many never recover from the offense. Usually, irreparable damage occurs when a Church is persecuted. How can the offender fully recover if those damaged cannot fully recover? The Lord is a just God. If you have done irreparable damage to His Kingdom, how can you go without consequence, even after you have repented?

Listen, don't say, "But I told the truth about them." In the Book of Numbers 12:1-15, didn't Aaron and Miriam speak the truth about Moses marrying an Ethiopian woman? Wasn't it true Aaron and Miriam heard from God too? It didn't matter to the Lord if they were telling the truth. The only thing that mattered was they were coming out against His servant. The Lord became angry, and Miriam became Leprous. Then to add to the situation, Aaron cried to Moses to plead with the Lord to heal her, and even though he prayed, Miriam still had to bear the consequences for seven days. What if Moses had not cried out to the Lord on her behalf? Miriam would have been a leper until the day of her death. Many do not realize the spiritual leader you have a problem with is the only one who can intercede on your behalf and ask the Lord to reverse the consequences. However, people are often too proud to repent and ask for forgiveness and prayer from those they accused. No, they have to keep up appearances all the days of their life. They will never say they were wrong.

Consider, in the natural, when you look for a job or career position. A wise job candidate is especially careful not to bad-mouth their previous employers in front of prospective employers. Then why are we not afraid to bash a Church and the brethren in front of others? If you are guilty of this, you need to repent! Pray: Lord, forgive me for my foolishness! Forgive me for hurting the saints! Listen, I have had several people who bashed me to others, come to me in a dream and repent to me. I do not believe they told others they were wrong, but I forgave them.

Now, reader, I will be the first to repent to you if you know me and feel I have done something to hurt you. Please, forgive me! But, I assure you, my heart's desire has always been to see you thrive. I desire to see souls saved. I desire to see people, in general, prosper. I wish to see you strong and diligent in your walk with the Lord. I assure you anything you perceived as wrongdoing was not intentional. Perhaps there was a misunderstanding of my purpose. I can honestly say I strive to follow the Lord in everything. If you look closer at the matter wherein you are accusing me, you will see the Lord was attempting to work in your character. Okay, reader, with that example, now is also a good time for you to start getting situations right with those you have wronged.

I admonish all who left a ministry because someone offended you or hurt your feelings to refrain from persecuting the Church with your mouth or otherwise. Keep your mouth from good and evil. Keep it from good lest you speak well with pretense and be found a liar before the Lord. Keep your mouth from evil lest you speak, sin, and suffer loss because of your actions. Genesis 31:29 declares, *"It is in the power of my hand to do you hurt: but the God of your father spake unto me yesternight, saying, Take thou heed that thou speak not to Jacob either good or bad."* Yes, because you are in pain, the power is in your hands to retaliate and do harm to the Church, but I caution you to forgive and let the Lord have His way. You only make yourself look bad when you try to bash a Church. Besides, when the Lord corrects a body of believers, they stand corrected.

James 3:2-18 reminds believers about the power and the consequences of the untamed tongue, *"For in many things we offend all. If any man offend not in word, the same is a perfect man, and able also to bridle the whole body. Behold, we put bits in the horses' mouths, that they may obey us; and we turn about their whole body. Behold also the ships, which though they be so great, and are driven*

84

of fierce winds, yet are they turned about with a very small helm, whithersoever the governor listeth. Even so the tongue is a little member, and boasteth great things. Behold, how great a matter a little fire kindleth! And the tongue is a fire, a world of iniquity: so is the tongue among our members, that it defileth the whole body, and setteth on fire the course of nature; and it is set on fire of hell. For every kind of beasts, and of birds, and of serpents, and of things in the sea, is tamed, and hath been tamed of mankind: But the tongue can no man tame; it is an unruly evil, full of deadly poison. Therewith bless we God, even the Father; and therewith curse we men, which are made after the similitude of God. Out of the same mouth proceedeth blessing and cursing. My brethren, these things ought not so to be. Doth a fountain send forth at the same place sweet water and bitter? Can the fig tree, my brethren, bear olive berries? either a vine, figs? so can no fountain both yield salt water and fresh. Who is a wise man and endued with knowledge among you? let him shew out of a good conversation his works with meekness of wisdom. But if ye have bitter envying and strife in your hearts, glory not, and lie not against the truth. This wisdom descendeth not from above, but is earthly, sensual, devilish. For where envying and strife is, there is confusion and every evil work. But the wisdom that is from above is first pure, then *peaceable, gentle, and easy to be intreated, full of mercy and good fruits, without partiality, and without hypocrisy. And the fruit of righteousness is sown in peace of them that make peace."* Figure 1 is a depiction of believers spewing gossip, throwing trash, and sowing discord in the Church. Where there is gossip, there is confusion, jealousy, and strife. The source of gossip is devilish; it is always spread by a demonic influence because the enemy aims to defile your character. Don't be a trash can for others; your soul is too precious to the Lord.

Figure 1. A depiction of Gossip in the Church

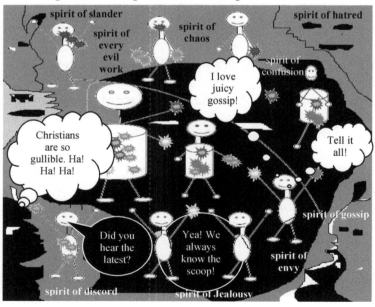

Reader, pray this prayer with me:

Abba, Father, in the name of Jesus Christ of Nazareth, I repent for speaking against Your servants. Please forgive me. There is so much I do not understand. Lord, ignorance is not bliss. I need Your mercy and wisdom to help me rectify the wrongs I have done. Show me all those whom I have wronged and injured with my tongue. Show me all those I need to go to and tell I was wrong. Give me the strength to explain to them that I did not discern You were purging me of those things that displeased You. Lord, prepare the hearts of those I have to approach to receive me. Grant me the courage and the grace to get things right in thy sight Lord. Jesus, if there is someone I cannot physically approach to repent to so I can correct my ways, please give them a dream of me repenting to them. Lord, please be my help and my strength to cooperate with the Holy Ghost as You complete Your work in me. Empower me to be steadfast in praying for the brethren instead of complaining and gossiping. In the name of Jesus, I pray. Amen!

CHAPTER SIX

ARE YOU BLESSED?

*"And they were offended in him. But Jesus said unto them,
A prophet is not without honour, save in his own country,
and in his own house."*

Matthew 13:57

One of the most prevalent forms of Church hurt is those in the congregation seducing married spouses. I would be writing amiss if I did not address this grave issue. In this chapter, I aim to enlighten, correct, edify, and comfort those who find it difficult to forgive that level of trespass. Accordingly, it is necessary to expose infidelity and teach spouses how to recognize an impending attack on their marriage.

I have seen a lot since I received salvation over twenty-four years ago. I have also personally experienced betrayal from people in the Church. And I have also seen others experience willful mistreatment from people they were supposed to trust. The Word of God declares in Matthew 18:7, *"Woe unto the world because of offences! for it must needs be that offences come; but woe to that man by whom the offence cometh!"* As I read and understand the Scriptures, I believe the Lord never intended believers to hurt one another. However, because the Church is full of sick folk who need a physician, we will inevitably hurt one another. Luke 5:31 declares, *"And Jesus answering said unto them, They that are whole need not a physician; but they that are sick."* Considering Scripture makes it easier to accept that we must experience some pain in our walk with the Lord, especially since folk in the Church are at different stages in their spiritual journey. However, when the offense is purposeful, perpetuated by someone who willingly and knowingly wrongs or harms you, the wrongdoing and the aftermath are more challenging to bear and forgive. It can also be incredibly challenging when you cannot communicate with the person peaceably to let them know how they've hurt and offended you. A lack of communication only compounds the situation and the associated pain. Moreover, suppose the offender feels no remorse or conviction for what they've done. In that case, it also amplifies the sorrow, lengthens the aftermath, and extends the healing process because they often continue to hurt you over and over again.

Living with a broken heart every day is a terrible way to live. The mind battles that accompany an offense can be devastating. And when there is a demonic element and influence, it will cause great depression and much strife until you are ineffectual. Then the pain of the offense begins to destroy your life. The longer you allow the wrongdoing to fester and eat at you, the more deeply rooted it becomes. The more deeply rooted, the more difficult it is for you to be delivered because it becomes a part of the very fabric of your character. To be free, at some point, you will have to commit to letting it go, repent for your unforgivingness, anger, and bitterness, and walk in the newness Jesus Christ died on the cross to give you.

The Word of God declares a lot about forgiveness, and Jesus said, don't be offended in the first place because once you are offended, it is difficult to forgive. The Books of Matthew 11:6 and Luke 7:23 both have a record of Jesus saying the exact words, *"And blessed is he, whosoever shall not be offended in me."* If you are not offended, you are blessed, walking in the forgiveness and healing power of God. If you are offended, you are unforgiving. If you are unforgiving, your sins remain. If your sins remain, then you are not blessed.

I'm telling you, when you don't let go of offenses, even in the case of infidelity, the pain in your heart and the brokenness of your mind will not allow you to have any peace, and you will not be able to prosper or move forward. You will even be unrecognizable to your loved ones. The only thing your spouse and children will see is someone acting crazy, literally crazy like you have lost all sense of sanity and reasonableness. You may have outbursts, often taking your pain out on others. You may go through crying spells, rage, and even plot to get revenge. Some people hold the hurt inside and don't air what they are going through, only to get sick physically. Others build an impenetrable wall, not allowing anyone else to get in to hurt or love them again. And some vow never again to trust, love, fellowship, or assist those of the household of faith. They promise never to labor in the Church, donate, marry, or attend a particular Church. Some even make a vow never to serve the Lord. Their life becomes a big book called *Never!* Some suffer in silence, which can be just as deadly as the outburst or open show of anger and bitterness. Silence is usually considered wise and virtuous. Yes, when the person is also quiet on the inside. However, if they are raging or hurt inside, there is no wisdom or virtue in silence; instead, there is a festering infectious disease waiting to rear its ugly head.

INFIDELITY AND FORNICATION

According to Divorce Magazine, 45 to 50% of married women and 50 to 60% of married men cheat on their spouses (Solomon & Teagno, 2018). Infidelity is one of the main reasons for divorce (Applebury, 2020b), so it is no surprise that the Church sees the effects of infidelity (Betts, 2020). Women are 69% more likely than men to file for divorce (Turvey, 2015). Unfortunately, I can honestly say I know more women who filed for divorce in my lifetime than men, and the Lord Jesus ordained many of those marriages.

There are many examples of offenses that cause deep wounds and bruises. Infidelity seems to top them all. It is challenging to release anger brought on by an affair, especially when spouses do not acknowledge their actions caused profound sorrow and distrust. It is also difficult to let go of anger if the cheating spouse blames the other spouse. I wholeheartedly believe the Lord arranges some divine marriages that no man should put asunder (Matthew 19:6 c-d only), even in the case of infidelity. Still, if a couple decides to reconcile their marriage instead of divorcing, it will be difficult to remain together unless the spouses' extramarital desires and struggles are resolved and extinguished.

Moreover, choosing to work on the marriage does not imply the adversary will not continue attempts to sever the union. Even some people in the Church will be vigorously working to bring the marriage to an end. That is when it gets hurtful indeed. When that happens, who can stand? You can stand! With the Lord on your side, you can get through whatever attempts to come against your marriage. *"I can do all things through Christ which strengtheneth me"* Philippians 4:13.

When a woman decides to leave her husband, she usually has at least one person encouraging her to end the marriage. The more people she has telling her to go, the easier her decision to leave will be. Sometimes the woman will have an external voice that sounds like an internal voice telling her to leave. If she chooses to listen to a voice that is not the Lord, she will miss the will of God. It is the same thing when a man decides to divorce. If he has another woman in his life, she will be the prominent force pressuring him to separate from his wife. I said force because women use sexual witchcraft to draw in the man's soul and control his decisions. The one operating in witchcraft will invite devils to speak softly to the husband concerning divorcing his wife. If the man is not vigilant in his relationship with the Lord, he just may fall for the trick. Those incantations and all soul ties have to be broken by the power of the Lord Jesus Christ.

Single Christians fit into different categories: those waiting for the Lord to send them a spouse and those not expecting a spouse. Sadly, some actively pursue married spouses to engage in affairs they hope will bring about a committed relationship. A survey of non-married women and men in the United States reported 53% of females and 60% of males admitted to "mate poaching." Mate poaching happens when a person attempts to entice someone in a committed relationship to abandon that commitment and begin a relationship with them instead. Mate poaching is prevalent in 30 other cultures besides America (Fisher, 2014).

The concept of mate poaching to find a spouse has been around a long time, but it rarely yields the fruit mate poachers desire, especially in the Church, because the Lord is actively fighting on behalf of marriages He has put together. Applebury (2020a) cited Dr. Jan Halper's book on successful men and reported no more than 3% of men who were unfaithful to their wives married their mistresses. Applebury (2020a) also cited marriage counselor Frank Pittman who said 75% of men who married their mistresses divorced them.

Nowadays, women feel comfortable approaching men to lay their claim. I know a married man who shared a story about a faithful sister in Christ who said to him while he was in Church: "Ooh, you are going to be my husband!" The man said, "Excuse me, Ma'am, what did you say?" She said, "You heard what I said. You are going to be my husband." The married man said, "I don't think so." She said, "Why not?" He said, "Because I am already married." She said, "I don't see a ring on your finger." Then he explained he takes it off while playing his instrument. "See, it's in my shirt pocket." At that time, he pulled the ring out of his shirt pocket and showed it to her, and she said, "I'm sorry, I repent, forgive me," and walked away embarrassed. Since it was a misunderstanding, the Lord immediately told the man to let her know there was no harm done. Unfortunately, some single women in the Church would not have cared that the man was married and would have continued to pursue him until he yielded to temptation. Some would have even started praying for the couple's union to fail, which is witchcraft that sends forth all manner of evil spirits to fight against the couple. Yeah, but we reap what we sow. That kind of attack will backfire!

On the other hand, there are men in the Church that seem to gravitate toward certain immature single women in the Church. Some of the men are married, and some of the men are single. They all have one line they speak in common to immature saints. The Lord said: *"You are going to be my wife."* English grammar states the Lord is speaking in the first person and announcing that the woman will be married to the Lord. She will be the Lord's wife, according to Isaiah 54:5. She is to consecrate herself unto the Lord. Unfortunately, when someone misinterprets the Word of the Lord, the woman or the man somehow believes the Lord is saying the two shall be married, even if one of them is already married. However, the Lord shared with me that the men are not lying, saying the Lord said something He didn't say, but the problem is misinterpreting what was said.

That type of confusion can become very painful because the wife doesn't know her husband is telling another woman in the Church that he will marry her. What does it mean for the wife, the marriage, and the children? Are they going to divorce? Is she going to die? Many men in the Church believe their wives will die, and they will marry someone else. While waiting for the marriage to end, the man and his purported future bride often start an unintended affair to the detriment of their walk in the Lord. And, with that type of trick, there is always someone else who validates it so the devil can carry on his deception unchecked for long periods.

The Lord told me the adversary is tricking many people into believing untruths. The men and women are ashamed to come forth and talk about it or admit their susceptibility. Therefore, many are unaware of the enemy's schemes. Why would the people of God be tricked in such a fashion? If you have spoken ill of someone else or have shown any amount of discontentment in your marriage, the Lord will allow many things to come upon you. Mainly the thing you said about someone else. In 2nd Chronicles 18:22, the Lord put a lying spirit in the mouth of all King Ahab's Prophets to trick Ahab into

99

going into battle wherein he would ultimately lose his life. The people who validate a trick of the adversary have lying spirits in their mouths.

Another explanation is the adversary has gained permission to try the marriage. The Book of Job reveals the accusatory tactics of the enemy. Once the trick is exposed, many are left confused about what happened. Is it even possible to recover from that level of a spiritual scheme? Yes, it is possible to recover. Armed with love and forgiveness and a desire to do the will of God, all involved can move on to brighter days. But, if the Lord's will is not allowed to prevail, there will be only misery for everyone. In those cases, remembering everything the Lord said to you concerning your spouse, marriage, and ministry will be indispensable. The Lord has not changed his mind concerning His plan for your marriage. All of that is a sign the marriage is in a battle. It's time to get up and fight for your marriage through prayer, fasting, and wielding the Word of God.

When a married couple enters a battle, one of the main things they will face is the spirit of seduction attempting to entice one of the spouses. Seduce means to persuade to disobedience or disloyalty; to lead astray usually by persuasion or false promises; to carry out the physical seduction of; entice to sexual intercourse; attract (MWCD).

The word lure is a synonym of the word seduce. So, based on the definition, when someone seduces another person, they do it via a devil. Yes, when seduction is going on, it is **always** by the power of a devil. Let me explain. Every time there is some form of seduction taking place, a devil is visibly present. Whether you can physically see it or not, it is there. Whether it be a single person speaking to another single person or a single person talking to a married person or two married people flirting with temptation, a devil is there trying to induce a seduction.

You will know if a spirit is trying to seduce you when you feel a strong sexual desire and lust in your loins or a strong urge to do something that is forbidden. That is especially true when the feeling will not go away until satisfied. And know that which is forbidden will always feel more pleasurable to the flesh because there is an evil spirit involved. Evil spirits aim to incite believers to disobey the Lord if they are single; they aim to provoke spouses to disloyalty. A spiritual person will recognize that it is a devil attempting to draw away their soul.

One time a supplier attempted to seduce me while I was at work. I knew he liked me, but I didn't think it was a big deal because I didn't like him. I thought it was only a business relationship, but apparently, he desired it to be more, even though he never told me. Plus, he was married and knew I was a Christian who wasn't dating. He knew I was waiting on the Lord for a Divine spouse. But, evil spirits don't care. Then, one day as I talked with him, a seducing spirit tried to entice me. As I left his presence to go back into my office building, I actually felt an unseen force surrounding me. I felt sticky all over, and I sensed unfounded flattery. I immediately knew what it was and began to rebuke the spirit in the name of Jesus. I said: "You foul spirit; you are not going to attach yourself to me. I command you to go back to the sender from whence you came in the name of Jesus." It all immediately stopped. From then on, I was watchful around that person. Shortly after that, the business relationship ended.

Again, one of the definitions of the word seduce is to carry out a physical seduction. When you look at the meaning of seduction, you find the words: temptation and charms. The definition of the word temptation is the act of tempting or the state of being tempted, especially to evil: enticement. A synonym of the word temptation is to lure. Now, we see the term lure for the second time. The definition of charm is the chanting or reciting of a magic spell: incantation; a practice or expression believed to have magic power; a trait that fascinates, allures, or delights; a physical grace or attraction; compelling attractiveness (MWCD). Have you ever heard the phrase: "They're charming?" Have you ever severed a relationship with someone and wondered what you saw in that person or what attracted you to that person? It was a charm.

Think about the seduction process. It includes decorating the flesh and the seducer using words to attract and draw away the one seduced. Again, the seducer's speech draws the person. The word allure means to entice by charm or attraction. Once more, there is the word charm. The Bible declares in James 1:13-16, *"Let no man say when he is tempted, I am tempted of God: for God cannot be tempted with evil, neither tempteth he any man: But every man is tempted, when he is drawn away of his own lust, and enticed. Then when lust have conceived, it bringeth forth sin: and sin, when it is finished, bringeth forth death. Do not err, my beloved brethren."*

You see, the adversary, through the power of seduction, provokes believers to yield to temptation. We submit as a result of our lust. So, it is not only the seducer who is guilty of seduction; it is the one seduced who also participates. While the flesh enjoys pleasuring itself, several bystanders are left wounded. Besides, the adversary plans to cause the believing seducer and the believing target to fall through disobedience to the Lord. Plus, if one of them is married with children, the nonparticipating spouse is left to deal with the aftermath and is in jeopardy of losing themselves and their soul because they find it challenging to deal with the situation graciously. The nonparticipating spouse not only feels rejected and insecure; they feel great uncontrollable anger or rage, and often, they become bitter. The enemy intends to cause the nonparticipating parties, including the children, to fall through Church hurt. Unforgivingness will cause a lot of people to forfeit eternal life.

It usually plays out like this: the seduction occurs; those caught in the seduction fall; the truth comes out in the open, and several individuals are left hurting. Fulfilling lusts of the flesh can have far-reaching consequences, like unplanned pregnancies that sometimes lead to abortions, spouses divorcing, displaced children, and failed visions for ministries. The Lord Jesus is then left to clean up the aftermath. It may take a long time to truly be delivered from sexual sins, especially if the two in adultery or fornication persist in the transgression. The Lord tests His children's hearts daily and gives many over to fulfill their desires and plans. The Word of God declares in Romans 6:23, *"For the wages of sin is death; but the gift of God is eternal life through Jesus Christ our Lord."* Jesus will forgive those who find themselves yielding to temptation. However, there is a price to pay for sin.

Furthermore, believe it or not, when these situations occur, it troubles the whole Body of Christ and is an occasion for the enemy to blaspheme the Lord's name. Additionally, it is challenging for a marriage to recover from adultery, and the adversary knows it, so it is a tactic used most often to bring down Christian marriages. It takes both people in the marriage desiring to do God's will to work through the situation. If the couple chooses to stay together and work through the crisis, they should expect an intense fight to save the marriage. Infidelity will be nothing compared to what will transpire as they mend and recover the marriage. Also, they should expect the seducer to continue attempts to draw away the spouse caught up in the seduction.

On the other hand, if the seducer, whether male or female, is unsuccessful in enticing the spouse, they may spread vicious gossip layered with lies about the situation. If that fails, they may plan to tell the nonparticipating spouse lies to cause them to leave the marriage covenant. I remember a person telling me someone was trying to seduce their spouse, and their spouse wouldn't yield to temptation, so the seducer said, "If you don't have sex with me, I'm going to say we did anyway. One way or another, you are getting a divorce." When there has been unfaithfulness in the marriage covenant, whether physical, mental, or emotional, the Lord must break the bond with the seducer. Yet, it must be the participating spouse's desire. They must also desire the will of God to come forth. Otherwise, the Lord's plan for the marriage will fail.

When the adulterer is a male, the Bible and the Strong's Concordance Hebrew Dictionary give a strong message in Proverbs 6:32, *"But whoso committeth (S.C. 5003) adultery with a woman lacketh (S.C. 2638) understanding (S.C. 3820): he that doeth it destroyeth (S.C. 7843) his own soul (S.C. 5315)."* In essence, that Scripture warns that those who yield to adultery's temptation renounce their beliefs and continually break wedlock. Why would anyone do that? Spouses often ask this unanswered question. The answer is spiritual and would be rejected by most. Yet, I will still give a Biblical answer.

When I dissect Proverbs 6:32, it reveals a man would break wedlock continually because he is destitute and void of character. He has no feelings, willpower, wisdom, or regard for himself or others. Having reached that point in his walk with the Lord, he needs to repent to receive a refreshing in the Holy Ghost. If the Lord Jesus

106

does not have mercy and help the one who has committed adultery, their soul will darken and come to ruin. They will suffer repeated blows and strikes from the adversary via mind battles, failed businesses, financial loss, and troubles. It is not uncommon for someone in adultery to incur excessive repair bills, illnesses, property loss, and more. Affairs are not about sex. The devil uses extramarital experiences to attack a person's entire life. The enemy will pound heavily and insistently on every area of a person's character to bring them under his power and control. The devil desires to make the transgressor feel abandoned and discarded by the Lord. His plan is for the family members and the brethren to give up on that soul. His goal is for the spouse to be so angry with the offender they stop praying for them. And when you stop praying for the offender, you stop praying for yourself. See, the enemy aims to corrupt the spouse, who is entangled. He plans to mar and waste their vitality, which will cause their soul to be in jeopardy. His goal is to cause them to perish utterly. If he is successful, the person will no longer desire to do the will of God, which will ultimately bring about eternal condemnation. Proverbs 6:32 is deep!

Furthermore, the Bible declares immoral women are a snare (Proverbs 7:5-27), and those who fornicate take the body parts of

Christ and make them the limbs of a harlot (1ˢᵗ Corinthians 6:15). Apostle Paul also said, *"Flee fornication. . . . For you are bought with a price: therefore glorify God in your body, and in your spirit, which are God's"* (1ˢᵗ Corinthians 6:18-20). The Scriptures admonish that adulterers, fornicators, and those who practice all sorts of sexual sins, including masturbation (Romans 1:26-27, Galatians 5:19-21, Colossians 3:5), shall not inherit the Kingdom of Heaven. The keys here are the phrases: "the natural use and inordinate affection." Both expressions emphasize unnatural lusts and desires; even those things that exceed reasonable limits are something that the Lord never meant for humans to indulge. The enemy's plan is for all souls to perish, so he must attempt to keep humans in a continual practice of sexual sins to ensure they are in that state when they pass from Earth to eternity, ultimately determining their eternal destination.

We must never forget the adversary's role in the matter of adultery. As I said before, sometimes the adversary petitions the LORD concerning those faithful in the Lord, and he gains permission to test the marriage. When there is a satanic influence in any situation, the believer will find it difficult to resist temptation. That is a spiritual sign the marriage is under attack. If you can't control yourself in a situation, it's spiritual. Period! If the spouses are not submitted to the

Lord's will for their lives in every area, a door is open for the enemy to come in and destroy the Lord's plan.

When infidelity and fornication cause people to be self-destructive, those involved are in an unhealthy place in their walk in the Lord, and divine intervention is needed. The Word of God gives useful insight into these situations. James 4:7 declares, *"Submit yourselves therefore to God. Resist the devil, and he will flee from you."* It sounds to me like it is not the Lord's will for the temptation to overtake us. However, if we have succumbed to temptation, all involved should repent, submit to the will of God for their lives, and take the necessary steps to resist the devil. Only then will the adversary flee. If we refuse to submit to the will of God, then we give place to the adversary to tear up more of the Lord's plan for our lives. The Word also instructs in Ephesians 4:27, *"Neither give place to the devil."*

Another issue is singles seducing other singles in the Church who find it extremely difficult to stop the cycle of fornication. There are often attempts by single women to force single men to marry them by getting pregnant. They may spread vicious lies about the other person to keep them from marrying someone else. After many years, I know of some single women who are still very angry because they

109

didn't get married after falling into sexual sin with someone. They felt deceived. In any case, they need to forgive the person and fight spiritually to keep immorality out of their lives.

Okay, let's wrap this up. You feel hurt by something you think is devastating, and it may be. But, tell me this, is it worth letting someone else's decision to sin ruin your walk with the Lord? Is it worth destroying all the Lord's plans for your life? Often, the perpetrators, who are sincere Christians, acknowledge their sin, repent, and those offended still don't forgive because there is so much pain. However, I admonish and encourage you to let it go right now, in the name of Jesus Christ of Nazareth!

You know the whole situation has put you in an unfruitful place in the Lord because you refuse to do the Lord's will and forgive. The Lord is in control. He allowed the situation to happen. In some cases, He orchestrated the situation. Because you will not forgive, you are now just as guilty as those who hurt you. That's deep! I'll repeat it. You are now just as guilty as those who hurt you! Did you hear me? You are now just as guilty of sin as those who hurt you! Process that for a moment.

You are more miserable now living with unforgivingness than you were when you heard the truth about the offense. You keep asking the Lord to heal you, yet it is not the offense keeping you sick. It is not the offense that is hurting you. It is you hurting yourself because you will not walk in the Scriptures and forgive. You refuse to forget. You still go crazy, even when months and years have passed and the offenders have corrected themselves. I am in no position to judge, yet I'm telling you to let it go. Stop thinking about it and don't tell another soul about it, not even the offender. Release it and watch your healing come forth. People are not perfect. As I said before, you have hurt people too and received forgiveness from the Lord. Now you must forgive as Christ forgave you, Colossians 3:13.

I hear someone saying, "BUT! If I forgive, they will be getting away with what they did to me, and that is not right!" Still, let them off the hook. Release them! You don't have to stay hurt, angry, or bitter, taking matters into your own hands, desiring revenge on others. If you pray for those who hurt you, you will feel a release, and it may cause the offender to repent. If you truly belong to Jesus Christ, you will love the one who hurt you. Love shall cover a multitude of sins (1st Peter 4:8).

What if you were the offender? Would you desire your sins to be covered? Yes, you would. Would you like the retribution of the Word of God upon your head for your sin? I think not. So forgive others and don't expect judgment upon them in return. Remember, the words the Holy Ghost inspired Apostle Paul to write in the Book of Colossians? *"Put on therefore, as the elect of God, holy and beloved, bowels of mercies, kindness, humbleness of mind, meekness, longsuffering; Forbearing one another, and forgiving one another, if any man have a quarrel against any: even as Christ forgave you, so also do ye"* (v. 3:12-13). The Lord is saying to forgive those who offended and hurt you, and I will forgive you for hurting my Kingdom!

To forgive means to pardon and release the offender from their trespasses against you. To pardon them is to liberate them from the penalty of the offense. Oh! It hurt to read that, didn't it? Yes! Release them, let them go free from the penalty, sentence, and imprisonment you have put them in, whether they acknowledged their sin and repented to you or not. If you don't forgive, you make yourself a judge. And James 4:12 declares, *"There is one lawgiver, who is able to save and to destroy: who art thou that judgest another?"* Jesus also addressed this exact situation in Scripture, *"He that is without sin among you, let him first cast a stone at her"* John 8:7 d-e only.

I understand it seems to the hurting party that the offender got off easy by repenting and asking for forgiveness, yet the argument is not valid. They didn't get off easy. They are hurting just as much as you, if not more, because the enemy comes in to cause guilt, condemnation, remorse, and all manner of spiritual attacks, especially if the perpetrators are sincere believers. When someone is in torment, there is no escape. Jesus is the only one who can help them. Surprisingly, if we fail a test by yielding to temptation, we retake the test. That can be troubling to the perpetrator as they may regularly fight ungodly inclinations and evil spirits. We all slip, especially if we have said or thought something about someone else. *"For all have sinned, and come short of the glory of God;"* Romans 3:23. The question to ask is: "Will we recover?" It depends on how we treated others when they fell. If we are merciful, we shall obtain mercy. If we are forgiving, we shall receive forgiveness.

Listen, I gave my life to Jesus when I was thirty years old. The devil immediately loosed his hold on me. The only thing I had to do was confess my sins, submit to water baptism in the name of the Lord Jesus Christ, and receive the gift of the Holy Ghost. The healing happened in a moment. I felt light, as if I was floating. All my sins and offenses were gone. I had a desire to make things right with a lot of people. Well, the Lord is ready to receive us now, just as He did when we first believed in His name and confessed our sins. The Lord's power forgives and heals in a moment, and we don't have to follow a ten-step plan. We must forgive others and repent for our unforgivingness. Then the Lord Jesus Christ will heal us. It is that simple. BUT! If we continue to dwell on the offense and not allow the Lord's principles to operate in our lives, the cycle of pain will continue.

1st John 1:9 declares, *"If we confess our sins, he is faithful and just to forgive us our sins, and to cleanse us from all unrighteousness."* After you confess your transgressions, the Lord will make you clean. He will purge and purify you (2511 Gk. S.C.). In cleansing, there are no more impure thoughts or words about past offenses or offenders. Your sanity and peace will return, and you will be able to dwell harmoniously with the saints again. Please understand that you become an offender when you don't forgive others who have trespassed against you. If you are an offender, you are displeasing the Lord. When you displease the Lord, you negatively impact your relationship with the Lord. So let us go on unto perfection and forgive, so everyone in the Body of Christ can heal.

Reader, pray this prayer with me:

Abba, Father, in the name of Jesus Christ of Nazareth, I recognize I'm in a terrible state. I have not forgiven those who have transgressed against me. In doing so, I have sinned against them and You. And I have not shown them the love of God they are due. I have not obeyed the Scriptures, which instructed me to forgive those who trespassed against me. I denied myself Your love and healing. Please, please, please forgive me. I do not take my trespass against You lightly because I know I'm in jeopardy of losing my salvation. I openly declare I forgive those who have trespassed against me, and I pray they will feel my forgiveness and love from this moment forward. Lord, in the future, help me to forgive quickly, in the name of Jesus. Amen!

CHAPTER SEVEN

OUTBURSTS OF ANGER

"An angry man stirreth up strife, and a furious man aboundeth in transgression."

Proverbs 29:22

CHAPTER 7: *OUTBURSTS OF ANGER*

Another form of deeply rooted hurt in the Church is when someone is angry. It does not matter why the person is angry, although the result will be the same: The person will always lash out at those around them. It is challenging to isolate anger and not commit some other form of sin with it. When humans are angry, they usually add to the outrage by acting on it in many different ways. Unfortunately, reacting angrily to any situation causes deeply rooted wounds for those caught in the web of someone's anger. *Better is the end of a thing than the beginning thereof: and the patient in spirit is better than the proud in spirit. Be not hasty in thy spirit to be angry: for anger resteth* [rest continually] *in the bosom of fools* (Ecclesiastes 7:9). When anger rests, it is in a seated position. It is there. There is no trigger. It does not need a reason to be angry; that is why we see many who respond with emotion or violence at the slightest disappointment or agitation.

While in a wrathful state, the mind processes many thoughts throughout the day, which feeds the anger, causing the angry person to become unseemly. Their outward behavior manifests through murmuring, complaining, verbal outbursts, physical altercations, throwing things, destroying property, malicious gossip, damaging others' reputations, and other vindictive behaviors. Getting angry is not a problem in itself because the Word of God declares in Ephesians 4:26, *"Be ye angry, and sin not: let not the sun go down upon your wrath."* However, misplaced anger is unfruitful and unwise. And when you don't put anger in its proper place, it becomes dangerous. I'm speaking of abnormal anger that operates daily. The kind of rage that is resentful, hateful, mean, and frankly hazardous to everyone. That type of anger is shortsighted and cannot see anything from anyone else's point of view. It is an anger that comes about from deeply rooted injuries and disappointments, and it is difficult to let go of because the person who has it begins to count on it for their very existence. Anger helps them feel secure. However, what they do not realize is they are angry with the Lord for allowing them to go through the situations they face. They are angry with Him because He will not change other people to suit them.

Conversely, it is a trick of the adversary because an angry person will not prosper in what they set their hands to do. Proverbs 22:24-25 declares, *"Make no friendship with an angry man; and with a furious man thou shalt not go: Lest thou learn his ways, and get a snare to thy soul."* The word snare is 4170 in the S.C. Hebrew dictionary, and it means a noose (for catching animals), a hook (for the nose), trap [bait]. So, anger baits the soul and grabs it, drawing it to the depths of Hell, like a trap catches an animal and brings it to its death. It is not easy to escape the wrath of an angry person. The enemy will make sure it is hard to get rid of anger so he can have an unlimited license to operate in the angry person's life.

In the Book of Proverbs, the Word of God warns us of the dangers of dealing with an angry person: *"As coals are to burning coals, and wood to fire; so is a contentious man to kindle strife"* (26:21). *"A continual dropping in a very rainy day and a contentious woman are alike"* (27:15*)*. *"It is better to dwell in a corner of the housetop, than with a brawling woman in a wide house"* (21:9). And *"It is better to dwell in the wilderness, than with a contentious and an angry woman"* (21:19). The Word of God is evident in declaring contentiousness destroys relationships, whether you are male or female.

How do you know if you are contentious? If you are likely to cause disagreements or arguments, you are contentious. If it seems like every time you turn around, you are involved in an argument, whether at work, home, or while you are out and about, you are contentious. If you do not have a problem confronting issues and are

121

willing to settle them, even if you have to yell to come to a resolution, you are contentious. If you believe any communication type is healthy communication, even yelling and name-calling, you are contentious. If you are in a place in your life where you cannot communicate without yelling, you are contentious and have a deeply rooted injury, which needs to be uprooted and healed.

Naturally, deeply rooted injuries take longer to heal than surface injuries. A wound goes deeper than a knick or scratch and is usually caused by violence, accident, or surgery. It is a laceration, which breaks through the skin, even if you have thick skin, and damages underlying tissues or organs. A wound can also affect you mentally and emotionally. When you are constantly arguing and yelling, it is a sign of emotional pain, both spiritual and natural. When your natural body is in pain, it is the body's way of telling you something is wrong. Well, when there is strife in your life, it is a sign of sickness in your character, which stems from emotional and social trauma. You know your character is sick when you start to do things you would not normally do.

You can feel a broken heart physically, mentally, and spiritually. Mentally you feel it when you think about your injury, and it causes you to cry or express anger. As long as you are not processing the situation through your brain, you feel normal. But as soon as you have a thought, not many, just one, emotional responses follow. When you have a severe spiritual injury, you cannot expect the offender or others to understand your pain or what you are going through. There is not a word you can speak to explain what you feel inside. Yet, we like to repeatedly communicate what's going on with us to the offender and others, hoping they will understand and provide comfort. Sometimes we think: If I can only get them to acknowledge they hurt me, I will feel better. Okay, they acknowledge it, then what? Do you let it go? Most of the time, you don't. You can't because the wound is so deep. One day you feel great, and the next day the anger starts all over again.

When you are in this condition, no one desires to console or fellowship with you. People say, "Should I leave you by yourself?" Unfortunately, when you are by yourself, the devil runs wild with your mind because you have many unanswered questions? Reader, I know you can relate to what I'm saying because to be by yourself is the first response of some going through serious injuries. However, a person who cuts off contact with others may be missing out on a support system and a lot of prayer opportunities. Anyone can be less contentious when they commune with themselves and the Lord, but the real test comes when you have to start communicating and fellowshipping with others again. It is not always good to leave the person to deal with that type and level of pain by themselves, lest they turn and hurt themselves. Oh, and many do.

Instead of spending time telling your business, ask the Lord if you can find a trustworthy and faithful individual to pray with you and for you so you can navigate your way through the situation. You do not have to tell what is going on to a person with a faithful spirit. You are only seeking more prayer power to add to your own. Remember, *"One man of you shall chase a thousand: for the LORD your God, he it is that fighteth for you, as he hath promised you"* (Joshua 23:10). *". . . If God is for us, who can be against us"* (Romans 8:31)? *"Nay, in all these things we are more than conquerors through him that loved us"* (Romans 8:37).

Think of additional prayer power this way; naturally, a person with a severe injury often needs someone to assist them with the wound. I have never seen anyone do heart surgery on themselves. You need a surgeon for heart surgery and preferably an expert. Jesus is the best therapist and surgeon you will ever know or encounter, and He is an excellent listener and counselor. He knows the whole truth and will tell you what you need to know and do to get through the season. So, extra prayer will be of great assistance. Besides, the Bibles teaches the power of two believers praying for an expected result: *"Again I say unto you, That if two of you shall agree on earth as touching any thing that they shall ask, it shall be done for them of my Father which is in heaven"* (Matthew 18:19).

Isaiah 53:5 declares, *"But he was wounded for our transgressions, he was bruised for our iniquities: the chastisement of our peace was upon him; and with his stripes we are healed."* Furthermore, Jeremiah 8:21-22 declares, *"For the hurt of the daughter of my people am I hurt; I am black; astonishment hath taken hold of me. Is there no balm in Gilead; is there no physician there? why then is not the health of the daughter of my people recovered?"* Whether you are a mature believer or a babe in Christ, Jesus is concerned when you are hurting. He is a balm for your wound. He took care of all our injuries at the cross. 1ˢᵗ Peter 2:24 declares, *"Who his own self bare our sins in his own body on the tree, that we, being dead to sins, should live unto righteousness: by whose stripes ye were healed."*

You may be saying: I am asking the Lord to heal me. I am asking the Lord Jesus to help me. I am allowing Him to do the work. All that may be true, yet you have to let your wound heal entirely

125

over time. How much time? I don't know. It depends on how the Lord Jesus plans to use your situation to help others. Why doesn't He do it in an instant? If He healed you in a flash each time you were injured, you would forget about the pain, and your character would not mature. The Word of God declares in Ecclesiastes 7:3, *"Sorrow is better than laughter: for by the sadness of the countenance the heart is made better."* According to the Vines, the heart is the man's character. If the Lord always healed you in an instant, you would not be available for His use to help someone else. A broken heart will motivate you to a spirit of compassion, grace, and mercy. You will be less judgmental. Life's hurts tend to eliminate pride. In our humility, we relate better to others going through the same situations.

Psalm 38:17 declares, *"For I am ready to halt, and my sorrow is continually before me."* I know you feel like giving up, but you can't give up. I know all the yelling and arguing is breaking you into pieces, yet you have to keep pressing your way until you get a breakthrough. In the Bible, King David felt many sorrows and deep wounds during his lifetime; that's how he wrote many of the Psalms for our benefit. In Psalm 116:3, he said, *"The sorrows of death compassed me, and the pains of hell gat hold upon me: I found trouble and sorrow."* Everything King David went through is helping us today. He was often on the run for his life and broken before God.

The thing about King David penning the Psalms is there was not always a specific occasion that inspired his writings and songs. Suffering and heartache were a way of life for him. He found solace in writing the Psalms and worshipping the Lord. The only way the great physician, Jesus Christ, can heal you is if you lie down in His presence and allow Him to do surgery on you. I've never seen anyone have surgery done while they were walking around or on a rampage. You have to be still for Him to complete the work in you. And keep in mind, only the Lord knows the day when the surgery will be complete, so don't go before Him one day and say, well, I did lie down in the Lord's presence, and it didn't work. Keep going before Him in humility until He blesses you like Jacob told the angel in the Book of Genesis 32:26.

When you need a healing from the Lord, lie prostrate before the Lord, repent of your sin and wrongdoing, and don't complain about what others have done to you. Pray Psalm 51:1-17 aloud, *"HAVE mercy upon me, O God, according to thy lovingkindness: according unto the multitude of thy tender mercies blot out my transgressions. Wash me throughly from mine iniquity, and cleanse*

127

me from my sin. For I acknowledge my transgressions: and my sin is ever before me. Against thee, thee only, have I sinned, and done this evil in thy sight: that thou mightest be justified when thou speakest, and be clear when thou judgest. Behold, I was shapen in iniquity; and in sin did my mother conceive me. Behold, thou desirest truth in the inward parts: and in the hidden part thou shalt make me to know wisdom. Purge me with hyssop, and I shall be clean: wash me, and I shall be whiter than snow. Make me to hear joy and gladness; that the bones which thou hast broken may rejoice. Hide thy face from my sins, and blot out all mine iniquities. Create in me a clean heart, O God; and renew a right spirit within me. Cast me not away from thy presence; and take not thy holy spirit from me. Restore unto me the joy of thy salvation; and uphold me with thy free spirit. Then will I teach transgressors thy ways; and sinners shall be converted unto thee. Deliver me from bloodguiltiness, O God, thou God of my salvation: and my tongue shall sing aloud of thy righteousness. O Lord, open thou my lips; and my mouth shall shew forth thy praise. For thou desirest not sacrifice; else would I give it: thou delightest not in burnt offering. The sacrifices of God are a broken spirit: a broken and a contrite heart, O God, thou wilt not despise." Often, we do not get the healing and peace we seek, expect, or need because we don't deal with our shortcomings. We are often too busy complaining about others' flaws. Lord, they did this to me and that to me. The Lord does not despise a broken and contrite spirit. Let's allow our inner man to be broken before God so He can have His way with us.

The Lord desires to use many of us to convert sinners, but the Church is so high we can't reach sinners. If the Lord is working on you, He plans to use you. If you are going through heartbreak, the Lord has a purpose. Brokenness before the Lord is not a bad thing. Again, Ecclesiastes 7:3 declares, *"Sorrow is better than laughter: for by the sadness of the countenance the heart is made better."*

With all that said, the yelling will not help the situation, yet it will lengthen the process, and you may lose some essential people in your life if you do not get control of your spirit during the healing process. *"And the servant of the Lord must not strive; but be gentle unto all men, apt to teach, patient, In meekness instructing those that oppose themselves; if God peradventure will give them repentance to the acknowledging of the truth;"* 2nd Timothy 2:24-25. I'm talking about the outbursts and how they ruin lives and plans because we cannot erase things we say. Some of you brought anger and discord into your relationship with Jesus, and even though Jesus initially healed you, you find yourself reverting to the old man, according to

Galatians 2:18. *"For if I build again the things which I destroyed, I make myself a transgressor."*

If emotional trauma continues to happen, the fabric of your character will change for the worst over time. And you will be difficult to fellowship with because you will be defensive. Additionally, any type of physical altercation, including so-called playful roughhousing, invites a spirit of violence into your relationships and home. Some people can take many insults, but it is challenging to cope with physical abuse, even if you do not strike back. In these situations, many prayers and personal reflection are needed. Through personal reflection, you will see it is not what the other person is doing to cause you to attack them. The attack is totally on you. One thing for sure is anger is at the root of the problem. Life's disappointments, previous failed relationships, or unforgivingness are usually the sources of such anger. If you are the abuser, I know from personal experience, the Lord Jesus is able to deliver you from anger and the evil spirits that incite you to take out your anger on others. And the Lord will heal you after you have been delivered. You must also forgive yourself. It will take you having a made-up mind to be renewed and released from the power of anger and unforgivingness.

If you are the one being attacked, forgive, and the Lord will heal you. The Lord will also show you that it is an evil spirit attacking you and not the person. If you love the person, you need to fight for their soul to be set free. If the Lord instructs you concerning the matter, follow His instructions. James 3:16 declares, *"For where envying and strife is, there is confusion and every evil work."* The Scriptures admonish us in Hebrews 12:14, *"Follow peace with all men, and holiness, without which no man shall see the Lord:"* To restore peace in your home, you have to kick these spirits out: envying, strife, confusion, and every evil work. Yes, these are the names of spirits, and you need to identify them and command them to leave your home in the name of Jesus Christ of Nazareth.

The only way these spirits can stay in your home is if they have an invitation to be there. So, not only do you have to forgive and forget, you need to fight in the spirit realm to take back the ground you have yielded to the devil. You must discern who and what you are warring against and kick those spirits out of your life. You will know the evil spirits are gone because the fruit of the Holy Spirit will reign in your heart. When the Holy Ghost reigns in your heart, He will also reign in your home. Galatians 5:22-26 declares, *"But the fruit of the Spirit is love, joy, peace, longsuffering, gentleness, goodness, faith, Meekness, temperance: against such there is no law.*

And they that are Christ's have crucified the flesh with the affections

and lusts. If we live in the Spirit, let us also walk in the Spirit. Let us

not be desirous of vain glory, provoking one another, envying one

another."

Reader, pray this prayer with me:

Abba, Father, in the name of Jesus Christ of Nazareth, I ask You to forgive me for being angry. I recognize the anger comes from the many deeply rooted issues I've held onto over the years. I'm ready to release all these issues and anger to You. I'm prepared to take up my cross and follow You, for I realize that not agreeing with Your plan for my life is the root of my anger. I forgive all those who have hurt me, intentionally and unintentionally. I pray they will forgive me also if I have injured them because I know anger hinders souls from seeing the love of Christ and being saved. If I hurt someone who is a believer, I pray You will strengthen them in their walk with You right now. If they are not a believer, I pray they will repent and give their life to Jesus. Lord, if it is Your will for me to contact the person and repent personally, show me who they are and what I did to hurt them. Now, I command anger to come out of my bosom and never return. I ask Lord that You will reverse all the damage I have done while in an angry state. According to Your will, mend all the relationships I damaged. Empower me to walk in the newness of life in Jesus' name. Amen.

CHAPTER EIGHT

TESTING THE MARRIAGE COVENANT

"And the LORD God said, It is not good that the man should be alone; I will make him an help meet for him."

Genesis 2:18

Every marriage will experience tests. In general, relationships will go through various ups and downs. Of a surety, life will try the marriage covenant to see what foundation it is standing on and what substance makes up the foundation. Tests and trials reveal the true reason the couple married and what expectations are predominant. Adversity will reveal the couple's character and whether they desire to do the Lord's will.

One morning in devotion, the Lord said to me, *"The Word of God holds the key to a blessed marriage. You will know the enemy's plan for your marriage by looking at the Lord's instruction for marriage in the Bible and the couple's marriage vows. No matter what the couple vowed, the enemy will use God's Word and their promises to each other to design his stratagem against the union."* Then the Lord began to show me how the enemy will incite married people to do the opposite of whatever the Lord has instructed them to do in the Word of God. Whatever vows they make, the devil will fight to make sure they cannot perform the vows. However, it is the Lord's will for the couple to fight for their marriage. The Lord told me to tell every reader of this book who is married or will be married: *"You made vows! Keep them! All you have to do is endure to overcome the enemy.*"

Ultimately, the devil plans to get souls into Hell, and if he can get married folk to violate all the things the Lord commanded, he will be successful in swaying the fate of those souls. According to the Book of Job 1:12, whenever the devil shows up in someone's life, he already has permission from the Lord to do what he will do, whether to hinder, tempt, or destroy. Your commitment to seek the Lord in prayer during that season must be greater than past times because that is the only way to be found standing by the power of God when the stormy season is over. During that time, your prayers will not necessarily stop what the enemy came to do because he has permission from the Lord, but it is to make sure you can stand against the wiles of the devil and withstand the promptings tempting you to give up.

Ephesians 6:10-18 instructs, *"Finally, my brethren, be strong in the Lord, and in the power of his might. Put on the whole armour of God, that ye may be able to stand against the wiles of the devil. For we wrestle not against flesh and blood, but against principalities, against powers, against the rulers of the darkness of this world, against spiritual wickedness in high places. Wherefore take unto you the whole armour of God, that ye may be able to withstand in the evil day, and having done all, to stand. Stand therefore, having your loins girt about with truth, and having on the breastplate of righteousness; And your feet shod with the preparation of the gospel of peace; Above all, taking the shield of faith, wherewith ye shall be able to quench all the fiery darts of the wicked. And take the helmet of salvation, and the sword of the Spirit, which is the word of God: Praying always with all prayer and supplication in the Spirit, and watching thereunto with all perseverance and supplication for all saints;"* When the enemy came to test me concerning my marriage, I needed the **armour of God** to stand in the battle. I would have perished without the **armour of God.** If the Holy Ghost had not strengthened me to persevere in prayer, I would not have maintained my resolve to serve the Lord. If I had not been obedient to everything the Lord commanded me, I would have lost the battle and changed the fate of my soul.

During that specific battle, I had to be mindful of every vision and dream the Lord gave me to ensure the will of the Lord would come forth. I had to earnestly pray for the will of the Lord to prevail and not my own will. When you resolve to do only the Lord's will, your prayers will be effective; and the Lord will fight on your behalf. However, if your prayers do not line up with the intention of God, you may find yourself fighting against the Lord, which is a battle you will lose. 1st John 5:14-15 declares, *"And this is the confidence that we have in him, that, if we ask any thing according to his will, he heareth us: And if we know that he hear us, whatsoever we ask, we know that we have the petitions that we desired of him."*

Based on what the Lord shared with me, the enemy's stratagem will look like the upcoming scenarios. It is the Lord's divine will for married couples to stay together and not divorce. So a couple will know the enemy is fighting against their marriage if they consider divorce when they have disagreements or arguments. If you think about what Jesus said in Matthew 19:3-8, you will understand the Lord is not the one driving couples to divorce: *"The Pharisees also came unto him, tempting him, and saying unto him, Is it lawful for a man to put away his wife for every cause? And he answered and said unto them, Have ye not read, that he which made them at the beginning made them male and female, And said, For this cause shall a man leave father and mother, and shall cleave to his wife: and they twain shall be one flesh? Wherefore they are no more twain, but one flesh. What therefore God hath joined together, let not man put asunder. They say unto him, Why did Moses then command to give a writing of divorcement, and to put her away? He saith unto them,*

140

Moses because of the hardness of your hearts suffered you to put away your wives: but from the beginning it was not so."

"For the woman which hath an husband is bound by the law to her husband so long as he liveth; but if the husband be dead, she is loosed from the law of her husband. So then if, while her husband liveth, she be married to another man, she shall be called an adulteress: but if her husband be dead, she is free from that law; so that she is no adulteress, though she be married to another man" (Romans 7:2-3).

Also, 1st Corinthians 7:10-11 declares, *"And unto the married I command, yet not I, but the Lord, Let not the wife depart from her husband: But and if she depart, let her remain unmarried, or be reconciled to her husband: and let not the husband put away his wife."* The Word of God declares a woman is bound to her husband as long as he lives, and he is not to put away his wife, and the wife is not to depart from her husband. So, if the original plan is for the couple to stay together for life, and the trials of life are inevitable, the Lord has the power and is willing to renew the couple's love and mend their wounded or broken marriage.

Unfortunately, instead of staying adhered like glue (cleaving), many couples separate or divorce. Why? The adversary uses all manner of tactics to beat upon the husband and wife until someone gives up. He fights them spiritually and works overtime to ensure they are distracted by life. When the couple is distracted, they are less apt to seek the Lord daily, so they are unprepared to overcome temptations and the relationship's hardships. However, there is nothing the couple will go through that the Lord cannot heal if they choose to cooperate and yield to the Lord's plan. Accepting God's will is often hurtful, but if one can muster the strength to continue trusting the Lord, there is a blessing at the end of the battle.

Couples need to decide early on in the marriage that divorce is not an option. Ask the Lord to help you work through every situation you will encounter. Consider how many people are fond of each other at the beginning of their marriage, and then later, they hate and despise each other? That change is often because the couple unknowingly enters a severe spiritual battle designed to destroy the marriage and what it represents.

Heterosexual marriage represents the relationship Jesus Christ has with the Church: a loving, forgiving, selfless, and sacrificial relationship. *"Wives, submit yourselves unto your own husbands, as unto the Lord. For the husband is the head of the wife, even as Christ is the head of the church: and he is the saviour of the body. Therefore as the church is subject unto Christ, so let the wives be to their own husbands in every thing. Husbands, love your wives, even as Christ also loved the church, and gave himself for it; That he might sanctify and cleanse it with the washing of water by the word, That he might present it to himself a glorious church, not having spot, or wrinkle, or any such thing; but that it should be holy and without blemish. So ought men to love their wives as their own bodies. He that loveth his wife loveth himself. For no man ever yet hated his own flesh; but nourisheth and cherisheth it, even as the Lord the church: For we are members of his body, of his flesh, and of his bones. For this cause shall a man leave his father and mother, and shall be joined unto his wife, and they two shall be one flesh. This is a great mystery: but I speak concerning Christ and the church. Nevertheless let every one of you in particular so love his wife even as himself; and the wife see that she reverence her husband"* Ephesians 5:22-33.

Scripture admonishes spouses to care for one another to a degree of love that will abolish all selfishness. When one eliminates selfishness, there is no room for many things a couple finds themselves facing. When someone in a marriage is selfish, adultery shows up. Selfishness causes disagreements about having children. Many couples do not agree on how many children to have or when to start. Having children will not be an issue if you let the Lord have His way in your marriage. Don't try to force it to happen. Don't try to prevent it. "Let the Lord *do* what He *do*." Argument solved.

When you hold on to selfishness, strife and abuse plague the marriage, arguments ensue about careers, education, major purchases, guiding the house, investments, and more. Love is a choice. Love positions the other person out in front of one's self. If you both become the least and a servant to the other, there will be no room for selfishness, and love and peace will abound in the marriage.

However, if one person is selfless and the other remains selfish, the marriage will be troubled and vulnerable to the adversary's attacks. If the couple is not on one accord, serving one another, the selfish one will not be content. Likewise, the one growing in love may come to feel resentment when their love is unreciprocated. Remember, love in a marriage must be unconditional. It is the only attribute needed to encourage the other person to submit to Jesus' will.

Proverbs 18:22 reveals another part of the Lord's plan for marriage, *"Whoso findeth a wife findeth a good thing, and obtaineth favour of the LORD."* The devil knows the man gains favor with the Lord when he marries. He knows the Lord will bless the work of the

144

man's hands. So, the enemy attempts to make the man look unprofitable and unfruitful in the eyes of his wife and children. Many wives feel insecure and give up supporting the husband and his God-given purpose and plans for the family. The devil also knows it is difficult to fight against the marriage if the couple prays with a common purpose. Therefore, a couple may continuously find themselves in situations that cause division. Jesus said, *"For where two or three are gathered together in my name, there am I in the midst of them"* (Matthew 18:20). Where the power of God is, the enemy cannot stay. He'll visit, yet he won't stay. The enemy has difficulty getting a foothold in a household when two or three people gather together on one accord in the Lord's name. Unity is a powerful weapon against the works of the devil.

Another blessing of the marriage covenant is for the couple to bring forth Godly children. Malachi 2:15 declares, *"And did not he make one? Yet had he the residue of the spirit. And wherefore one? That he might seek a godly seed. Therefore take heed to your spirit, and let none deal treacherously against the wife of his youth."* The enemy will use specific Scriptures to design stratagem against the couple to prevent them from being fruitful. Many believers are in a spiritual battle concerning having children. Sometimes, the lack of fruit has nothing to do with the Lord or the couple. The adversary sends forth all manner of witchcraft against the couple to rob them of their fruit. That is why many married couples have miscarriages and stillbirths. Also, sometimes the Lord has a particular plan for the fruit the union will bear. In these cases, the woman will not have children until the proper season, like in the Scriptures with Isaac, Esau & Jacob, Joseph, Samson, Samuel, and John the Baptist.

Furthermore, if the couple does bear fruit, their children often encounter many difficulties and struggle with whether they desire to serve the Lord when they are adults. The Bible declares in Proverbs 22:6, *"Train up a child in the way he should go: and when he is old, he will not depart from it."* In any case, remember: The Lord made humans fruitful, and He does not usually interfere with the reproductive process. Everything the Lord made to reproduce will reproduce. However, if you find you are barren and it is the Lord's will for you to bear fruit, then you may be in a spiritual battle designed to compel you to give up on your marriage before your blessing comes forth. Seek the Lord to find out the category you fit in and pray accordingly.

Here is another trick. In many Scriptures, the Lord instructed wives to obey their husbands. In truth, He gave several charges to

146

women in Titus 2:3-5, *"The aged women likewise, that they be in behaviour as becometh holiness, not false accusers, not given to much wine, teachers of good things; That they may teach the young women to be sober, to love their husbands, to love their children, To be discreet, chaste, keepers at home, good, obedient to their own husbands, that the word of God be not blasphemed."* With that charge in mind, the enemy will incite women, even the most faithful of the Lord's handmaidens, to do the opposite of what the Scriptures declare. That is why we have women leaving home to work for earnings without the husband's consent. The household, including the husband and the children, are left to fend for themselves. And as my husband teaches: "The dads and moms are misplaced. The children are confused and displaced, and many are improperly cared for because there is no one to keep the home or guide the house." Proverbs 29:15 declares, *"The rod and reproof give wisdom: but a child left to himself bringeth his mother to shame."*

The couple should talk and agree on everything. Wives, if your husband says no, take it as the Lord Jesus saying no. Allow your husband to be the man and learn his place under the Lord's guidance. Husbands, if the wife is uncomfortable with something you believe the Lord is telling you to do, reconsider and ask the Lord again. If you are sure of the Lord's instructions, pray for your wife! Wives, don't get angry if your husband disagrees with you. Just pray and let the Lord speak to him! Husband's while you are asking the Lord, remember Matthew 27:19. *"When he* [Pontius Pilate the governor] *was set down on the judgment seat, his wife sent unto him, saying, Have thou nothing to do with that just man* [Jesus Christ]*: for I have suffered many things this day in a dream because of him."* Don't make a move until the Lord says, *"Yes."* As you two grow in the Lord, the process will get easier as you both learn to trust the Lord and each other. Note: this counsel is for immature couples. Mature couples already know to operate in the Word of God.

Additionally, women are no longer discreet and chaste. Being considered a lady is an insult. They no longer teach good things. Instead, women are teaching other women to do what makes them feel good. Women who do not operate in the Word of God will tell women: "Girl, I would leave him. I wouldn't take his mess. You have to look out for yourself." What about my children? "They'll adapt." All of that is terrible counsel; there are ramifications for the one who listens and follows incorrect, ungodly, unscriptural counsel. Proverbs 31:10-12 clearly defines the character of a virtuous woman: *"Who can find a virtuous woman? for her price is far above rubies. The heart of her husband doth safety trust in her, so that he shall have no need of spoil* [riches]. *She will do him good and not evil all the days of her life.* For example, women, it is your husband's duty to correct you when you are wrong. Just as Jesus corrects those that belong to Him, your husband will correct you. If he loves you, he will correct you. Instead of receiving correction from our husbands with the right attitude and spirit, we disagree, murmur, and complain.

Sometimes we even speak against our husbands to others, doing him evil instead of good. But what we do not realize is it is the Lord requiring that thing of us. When we disagree with our husband being our head, we strengthen our rebellion and prove that the Lord cannot trust us with greater responsibilities in His Kingdom. The Word of God declares, *"For whom the Lord loveth he chasteneth, and scourgeth every son whom he receiveth. If ye endure chastening, God dealeth with you as with sons; for what son is he whom the father chasteneth not? But if ye be without chastisement, whereof all are partakers, then are ye bastards, and not sons."* (Hebrews 12:6-8).

Moreover, women are not teaching other women to obey their husbands. The adversary's plan is to have women ignoring and disobeying the Word of God, and it has far-reaching consequences, which may affect the eternal destiny of generations of people. How

149

can anyone get into Heaven when they do not obey the Scriptures? The Scriptures will judge us!

Colossians 3:19 is another Scripture the adversary commonly utilizes to construct the downfall of a marriage. *"Husbands, love your wives, and be not bitter against them."* Many husbands are angry and bitter against their wives, and they do not know the reason. Why would the devil try so hard to cause a husband to be bitter against his wife? His goal is to hinder the husband's prayers because there is great power in his prayers, especially if he is a man of faith and authority. 1st Peter 3:7 declares, *"Likewise, ye husbands, dwell with them according to knowledge, giving honour unto the wife, as unto the weaker vessel, and as being heirs together of the grace of life; that your prayers be not hindered."*

The devil has been successful in getting men to stop praying. Frankly, women in the Body of Christ pray more than men do. However, if men would pray, they would be more effective in foiling the enemy's plan against the Church, the marriage covenant, and the children. Distractions and no prayer life explain why many leaders in the Body of Christ fall. The enemy is cunning to strike when the saints are weak. It's like a natural enemy who comes at a time of vulnerability; he does not strike at a time when his foe is strong and expects something to happen. No, he comes when their guard is down. He stirs up trouble when they are not paying attention. Unfortunately, many of the enemy's plans are plotted long in advance.

For example, my husband prays a lot. At the beginning of our marriage and ministry, we were not aware of the level of demonic activity fighting against us. After many years of prayer and misunderstandings, the Lord revealed the adversary's plan. My husband has often come to me and told me the adversary was trying to get him to be angry with me. At the same time, the adversary was continually trying to make me regret being married. When these events would happen, my husband knew it was the adversary because there was no cause for how we were feeling. My husband finally started asking the Lord, "What is the purpose in the adversary trying to get me to hate my wife?" Then the Lord revealed to us the devil was trying to hinder my husband's prayers.

We know my husband's prayers make a global difference in the spirit realm because we have seen the evidence when his prayers and decrees come to pass. If his prayers were not effectual, the enemy would not waste time trying to hinder them. *"Confess your faults one to another, and pray one for another, that ye may be healed. The effectual fervent prayer of a righteous man availeth much"* (James 5:16). If men would just pray and lead their families and Churches in prayer, we would see a mighty move of God!

The enemy also listens to our desires and plans, then proceeds to devise stratagem to foil, delay, or hinder our efforts. I knew a believing couple ordained by the Lord to be together. We noticed everything they were excited about in the Lord, including their marriage, were the very things causing strife. Now, after many years, we know it was the adversary riding their backs to foil the Lord's plan for the marriage. They were not aware it was the adversary, so they did not rebuke the thoughts the devil inserted into their minds or cancel the words he incited them to speak. I know of many similar stories, which all ended with divorce. All of those couples had callings, and the enemy successfully hindered the Lord's plan for their lives.

Husbands have considerable authority to pray, but many are not warring to match their spiritual battle. Many wives also have weak prayer lives. Prayer is the key. Both spouses and the children need to have dedicated time to pray because it is more important than they know. Everything else that seems important is not as important as it seems, not even a little bit. The devil will relentlessly attack your marriage and family when prayer is not a priority in the household. He will even attack your Church when there is a lack of earnest prayer.

Do not despise prayer. Each person in the household should start 15 minutes of morning devotion to listen to the Lord. Intercede at home daily. Participate when your Church has intercessory meetings. You must spend a lot of time in the Lord's presence to overcome a spiritual attack on your marriage. Note that a spiritual attack may come from someone continually trash-talking you, your spouse, or the Church. Gossip sends forth evil spirits to attack and puke on people.

My husband and I have seen attacks on marriages with our own eyes. We understand the effects of a weak prayer life. When spouses and children don't pray for one another, all hell will break loose in their lives and their ministry. Yes! Children need to learn how to effectively and adequately pray for their Church, parents, schoolmates, neighbors, and those in authority. The whole house must pray! If you genuinely desire to do the will of God, it is time to stop fighting each other and fight the adversary in the spirit realm. Families who war in unity soar in unity. You cannot move forward divided. The Lord puts couples together to be a guard for each other against the enemy. When prayer ceases, you let your guard down, and you give the enemy a license to infiltrate and destroy the vision the Lord has for your life. Remember, there is no substitute for prayer. There is no substitute for activating the power of Jesus Christ in our lives. That is why 1st Thessalonians 5:17 declares, *"Pray without ceasing."*

A PERSONAL MESSAGE TO WIVES

I know sometimes you may feel like giving up on your marriage and the ministry the Lord has called you to, and you may be experiencing some form of Church hurt. However, leaving your husband or the Church is not the answer. Contrarily, if you follow that frame of mind, you will be fulfilling the enemy's plan for you to cease doing the will of God. It will also give the Lord's enemies an occasion to blaspheme His name. Frankly, you will be wide open for the enemy to take your natural life.

So, what should you do when you experience neglect, abuse, or ridicule by people in the Church? What should you do in cases of marital infidelity, whether perpetrated by your spouse or you? What should you do when you feel isolated from the saints? What should you do when your family experiences financial woes? What should you do when women in the Church falsely accuse you or misunderstand your intentions? What should you do if your husband is bitter against you? Pray! Pray! Pray! Pray and pray again!

Unfortunately, many wives leave their husbands instead of staying and fighting the true enemy attempting to destroy the family. Again, there is an evil force that actively fights against all marriage covenants because it is the most remarkable institution established by the Lord. That is why infidelity is commonplace in many marriages in the world today, because the devil knows the significance of the marriage bond and how much damage he can do to a household if he infiltrates the relationship.

Many Christian wives love the Lord, so they live through and tolerate betrayal, vicious gossip, jealousy, and hatred from other women who envy their lifestyle. Jesus said, *". . . Love your enemies, bless them that curse you, do good to them that hate you, and pray for them which despitefully use you, and persecute you; That they may be the children of your Father which is in heaven: for he maketh his sun to rise on the evil and on the good, and sendeth rain on the just and on the unjust. For if ye love them which love you, what reward have ye? do not even the publicans the same? And if ye salute your brethren only, what do ye more than others? do not even the publicans so? Be ye therefore perfect, even as your Father which is in heaven is perfect"* (Matthew 5:44-48).

So, instead of retaliating, the believing wife must pray for those who come out against her. She should pray that they correct themselves and be strengthened in the Lord because the Lord would have all men to be saved. She can't afford to see people as enemies since she never knows what the Lord is doing in someone's life. Nevertheless, that mistreatment from Church members can cause a wife to struggle in her walk with the Lord. She struggles due to the saint's under-appreciation of her untiring work to help them. Some churches even carry on as if she does not labor to enable the ministry to move forward. Well, I'm here to tell you, humans may not acknowledge your sacrifices, but the Lord knows them all. Believe it or not, the Lord is in control of your life, not humans.

Wives who are in these and other unpleasant situations need to cleave to the Lord through the Word of God. Cleave to the Lord in prayer, praise, and worship. Fast from food if you can. Set aside time to spend with the Lord in a private place, and by doing so, He will share with you His plan for your life. He will give you peace. But you must trust the Lord! It may seem difficult to bear your specific circumstance, but peace will come, and you will have a new outlook on life. Let the Lord rescue you instead of your family, friends, and associates. When you run to others, instead of the Lord, you will never find the peace you are really seeking. The Lord is truly your only refuge!

Wives experience discouragement because they have put the Church, husbands, children, and family in front of their relationship with the Lord. Many wives don't realize they have neglected their relationship with the Lord since they are always busy guiding the house, taking care of the husband, taking care of the children, and taking care of the needs of the children of God in the Church. They believe they are nurturing their relationship with the Lord by doing all these things for others. However, it is not so, and it opens a door for you to become discontent in your marriage. You need to care for your relationship with the Lord, aside from your labor in His Kingdom.

Now, what I am about to explain is real, and it is for your good. The Lord will allow your relationship with your husband and the Church to come crashing down to draw you closer to Him. The truth is the Lord is not angry with you or punishing you. Again, He is drawing you closer to Him, but you are not connecting the signs. When you only focus on keeping your family together, you will find yourself kicking against what the Lord is trying to do in your life.

You may also be striving about keeping your position in the Church instead of staying close to Jesus. If you stay close to the Lord and do what He requires of you, He will keep the family together if it is His will.

Again, the Lord is not punishing you. I'll repeat it. He has a plan to draw you closer to Him. The Lord desires a deeper relationship with you. You know you have not been praying, worshipping, or reading the Word of God like you should or like you desire. You are in such an uncertain place in your walk with the Lord that you can't even believe the good things the Lord says about you or says to you. I have learned if someone, anyone, can come and tell you something about you that is not true, and you believe it as if it is the truth, knowing that it is not, then you are not in the right spiritual state. You should only believe and receive what the Lord says about you, good or bad.

Once more, the Lord is concerned about you if you have neglected yourself. It seems like what you are going through is the hardest thing in the world to go through, but it is working for your good and the Lord's purpose. *"And we know that all things work together for good to them that love God, to them who are the called according to his purpose"* (Romans 8:28). Get back in the Word of

God and get into the Lord's presence, and He will reveal His plan to you. His plan for you may be hard to believe or accept when you feel oppressed. However, rest assured, His purpose is what is best for you.

Readers of this book, the Lord told me to tell you He does have good things in store for you. The Word of God declares in 1st Peter 5:7, *"Casting all your care upon him; for he careth for you."* You must believe, first and foremost, the Lord is not angry with you. He continually cares for you. He knows your end from the beginning. The Bible declares in Isaiah 46:10, *"Declaring the end from the beginning, and from ancient times the things that are not yet done, saying, My counsel shall stand, and I will do all my pleasure:"* He knew you and sanctified you before He formed you in your mother's womb. *"Before I formed thee in the belly I knew thee; and before thou camest forth out of the womb I sanctified thee,"* Jeremiah 1:5 a-b only. The Lord knew you would be in the place you are in right now in your life. He is not surprised by what you are going through. He is not surprised by your hurt or by your so-called craziness. You have to remember you are valuable to Him, and there is a purpose for everything happening in your life.

Those who are more emotional by nature cannot always control their emotions when they are in great pain. Usually, deep pain pierces the heart like a dagger. If a woman does not feel secure in her relationship with the Lord, she will not feel confident in her relationships with her husband or the Church, and no one will be able to rely on her service. Women need to feel secure. Otherwise, their insecurities will cause them to experience extreme distress, which will be a catalyst to unhealthy behavior.

The enemy's plan entails the false belief that the Lord is angry with you, so you will stay out of the Lord's presence and not repent and worship the Lord. The adversary's plan is for you to believe the Lord does not hear your prayers, and all your efforts to reconcile your relationship with the Lord are in vain. The devil's scheme is for you not to pray because when you get in a vein of prayer, the Lord will reveal His more excellent design for your life. He will reveal answers to some of your questions. The Lord will even show you the evil spirits trying to destroy your home. And He will empower you to pray for your family and break the yoke of the enemy.

The enemy proposes to keep you feeling helpless and hopeless, so you will not fight against the powers of darkness. Furthermore, the enemy's plan is for you to be afraid to read the Word of God because Scripture is convicting. However, I admonish you to read the Word of God. Let it convict you and renew your mind. Let it transform you from a worldly mindset to the Mind of Christ. When you have a worldly mindset, your thoughts will counsel you to your detriment, but when you have the Mind of Christ, the Lord is your counselor for your good (1st Corinthians 2:16). If you had a close walk with the Lord at one time in the past, get back to that place. Then go deeper in your walk with the Lord. It is the only solution to what you are experiencing as a wife. The Bible declares, *"For as he thinketh in his heart, so is he:"* Proverbs 23:7 a-b only.

One word of caution, you are not seeking the Lord to fix your situation. You are seeking the Lord so you can be renewed and healed. Most of all, you desire to strengthen your relationship with the Lord. That alone will help you see clearly, and you will experience a breakthrough. The time you spend with the Lord is for you, so keep your eyes and mind on Jesus. As well, you are not seeking the Lord, so you can go back to who you were before the trouble started because that person is the one the Lord is reshaping into a new person. Remember, you are always on the Potter's wheel. So, don't get comfortable. Keep an open mind so the Lord can bring to pass His plan in your life.

A PERSONAL MESSAGE TO HUSBANDS

This section was written very carefully and with the counsel of my husband. Unfortunately, many men in the Church also fail to see their real enemy and often blame their wives and the Church for their marital problems. The truth is the adversary is behind the evil thoughts you have against your wife and the Church. You must spend a lot of time praying for your wife. Only then will you see her true worth and beauty. You also may be experiencing anger and a desire to give up walking with the Lord altogether. However, I admonish you to hold on to the Word of God because *"All scripture is given by inspiration of God, and is profitable for doctrine, for reproof, for correction, for instruction in righteousness: That the man of God may be perfect, throughly furnished unto all good works"* (2nd Timothy 3:16-17).

Read the Bible daily, and it will make you perfect, and the works of your hands will prosper as you obey the Lord and walk in the Scriptures. Walking in the Scriptures is profitable for you! If you could see what the Lord has in store for you, you would not spend time blaming others for your problems. 1st Corinthians 2:9 gives a clue that He has planned great things for those who endure to the end, *"But as it is written, Eye hath not seen, nor ear heard, neither have*

162

entered into the heart of man, the things which God hath prepared for them that love him." Consequently, let's address some common issues husbands face in the Church.

Firstly, husbands may feel their wives put the Church in front of them by spending more time at the Church than at home. For instance, I once had a sister come to me when I was a single sister in the Church and ask me if she should spend New Year's Eve with her husband instead of singing with the choir at the Church's watch night service. I always believed the Lord had her confide in me because we barely knew each other. During that season, I spent a lot of time with the Lord, and He used me to minister to others with accuracy.

Anyway, although her husband was not a believer, she informed me he had been very loving and cooperative about her spending time at the Church. Yet, he had a problem with her spending all of the special occasions and holidays with the ministry. His desire was for her to stay home with him and their son to bring in the New Year. She wondered what to do. She advised she had been praying about it and felt she needed to stay home with her husband but was afraid to tell the music Minister. I responded, "If I were you, I would spend time with my husband. Just let them know you will not be able to participate. Since you have been faithful during all the other holiday events, it should not be a problem. Just go talk to him."

From my perspective, as an unmarried woman, single women are waiting on husbands, and here was a woman with a loving husband who was on the verge of jeopardizing her marriage so she could please someone other than her husband. She was afraid to tell the music Minister she would not sing with the choir. The Minister of music was not a tyrant or an unreasonable person. However, there was some confusion on her part as to her responsibility to her husband.

In 1st Corinthians 7:32-34, Apostle Paul explains, *"But I would have you without carefulness. He that is unmarried careth for the things that belong to the Lord, how he may please the Lord: But he that is married careth for the things that are of the world, how he may please his wife. . . . The unmarried woman careth for the things of the Lord, that she may be holy both in body and in spirit: but she that is married careth for the things of the world, how she may please her husband."* Thankfully, she took the Holy Ghost's counsel, requested the evening off, and spent time with her family. Shortly after, her husband started coming to Church and gave his life to Jesus. She soon became pregnant again and then again, bearing two more sons. If she hadn't used wisdom, her husband would have felt he had no recourse because it would have appeared as if the Church was fighting against the marriage.

Apostle Paul also declares in the Book of 1st Timothy 5:14, *"I will therefore that the younger women marry, bear children, guide the house, give none occasion to the adversary to speak reproachfully."* That Scripture clearly explains marriage's divine order, which is for the wife to guide the home. When wives are not in their proper place in the Lord and refuse to listen to their husbands' counsel, they open a door for the adversary to infiltrate the marriage.

Ephesians 4:27 declares, *"Neither give place to the devil."* That Scripture is announcing to the believer, do not give, grant, bestow, bring forth, or deliver up an opportunity, license, or room for Satan, the false accuser, to use against a believer in any wise. It takes wisdom and empowerment from the Lord to be married. The Bible is clear concerning the matter, and Churches should teach wives the truth; they must obey and reverence their husbands. Ephesians 5:22 urges, *"Wives, submit yourselves unto your own husbands, as unto the Lord."* Once more, Ephesians 5:24 and 33b instructs, *"Therefore as the church is subject unto Christ, so let the wives be to their own*

165

husbands in every thing. . . . and the wife see that she reverence her husband."

When the Lord says your wife is to be in subjection to you concerning everything, even as the Church is subject to Christ, he means that literally. What a lot of people do not understand is that particular Scripture implies and suggests the husband is like a ***god*** to the wife as Moses was to the Children of Israel; Aaron was his Prophet – a similitude of Christ and the Church leaders today. She must obey her husband in the same way she would obey the Lord. Like Sarah was with Abraham. She even called him lord. That is a great responsibility for the husband to bear, and most are not up to the task since they often abuse it, not realizing the Lord is watching because the wife is an heir of salvation. Truthfully, you both are heirs together of the grace of life (1st Peter 3:7). That means you are responsible for your wife's well-being, and if you do not correct her and let her do her own thing, you are showing the Lord you do not love your wife, nor do you love Christ. You will give an account to the Lord for how you love your wife. And know this: You cannot force her to be in subjection to you. She must trust you. You have to win her over with love so that she will voluntarily submit to you. Teach her the Scriptures at home because she sits under your tutelage

(1st Corinthians 14:35). Once the Lord's plan is unveiled, she will gladly submit to you because she will be motivated to please the Lord; that is if she desires to prosper and ultimately receive eternal life.

Furthermore, Colossians 3:18 also admonishes, *"Wives, submit yourselves unto your own husbands, as it is fit in the Lord."* So, no matter what the Church requires of a wife, she is obligated to ensure her husband supports her ministerial responsibilities. Wives must remember the Scriptures declare it is proper and suitable for wives to submit to their husbands. When a wife knows the Scriptures, these types of misunderstandings resolve quickly.

Secondly, a believing husband may feel his wife listens to the Church leader instead of listening to him. It becomes a delicate situation because, on the one hand, the Word of God commands in Hebrews 13:17 to *"Obey them that have the rule over you, and submit yourselves: for they watch for your souls, as they that must give account, that they may do it with joy, and not with grief: for that is unprofitable for you."* On the other hand, the Word of God also instructs the woman to obey her husband. When there is a conflict between the two, what should a woman do?

For example, I remember a believing brother full of the Holy Ghost, sharing with me someone in the Church was continually counseling his wife to do the opposite of what he was instructing her to do. Again, the Word of God is straightforward concerning this matter: The wife is to obey her husband. If the husband is wrong, then the Lord knows how to correct him. 1st Peter 3:1 encourages, *"Likewise, ye wives, be in subjection to your own husbands; that, if any obey not the word, they also may without the word be won by the conversation of the wives;"*

The husband should cleave to and love his wife, and she is to love and reverence her husband. Cleave in Matthew 19:5 means to glue upon, to stick to, and to join self closely. If there is a problem or misunderstanding regarding instruction from the husband, the wife should talk to her husband. If the wife finds it difficult to agree with her husband, she should follow Scripture and pray for unity in the home. If she still believes something is wrong, they would have to agree to get counseling from the spiritual leader to resolve whatever particular issue they might have. Personally, I believe problems between the husband and wife should be resolved through prayer and seeking the Lord for His counsel on the matter. But if one of the two refuses to be obedient to the Lord's counsel, that's when they get a spiritual leader involved. It is a way to force someone to obey, and usually, it does not turn out well.

Consider, if the husband has not received salvation and the wife brings a marital issue before the leader or the marriage counselors instead of talking to her husband. She is closing the door on any possibility of her husband giving his life to Jesus. Moreover, if her husband is a believer, she is bringing division into the Church. If the wife has yet to receive salvation, then the Pastor should go forth in prayer for the woman to confess her sins, of course with her consent. A spiritual Mother in the Church should then teach the woman the Scriptures and her responsibility to her husband and children.

A Church cannot repair marital problems. However, it can reinforce to the husband and wife what the Scriptures declare. The Church leaders can also pray for the couple, yet the work has to be put in by the couple, and they have to depend on the Lord to keep the marriage, especially if the Lord put the two people together. By seeking the Lord, the couple will understand why the Lord put them together and what His plan is for the marriage. If they both desire to do God's will and please the Lord, He will help them recover the marriage. I'm speaking from experience.

There have been women seeking counsel about their husbands, but no one should get counsel about their marriage unless both spouses are present. It protects the couple and the counselor from misinformation. I remember a story of a sister who desired to divorce her husband. She threatened to divorce him several times. Then she started insisting the Lord told her she could divorce her husband. The Lord does give people over to their desires. Thankfully, sometimes the likelihood of divorce causes the couple to see the value of staying married. Her husband started trying to correct himself. But, the sister was so hurt and angry; she could no longer see to repair the marriage. Then he began to blame the Church for his failed marriage. He expected the leaders to tell his wife she could not divorce him. No one can stop people from doing what they desire to do. 1st Corinthians 7:15 declares, *"But if the unbelieving depart, let him depart. A brother or a sister is not under bondage in such cases: but God hath called us to peace."* Only the Lord can intervene once a person has made up their mind about something, yet He will not force anyone to stay in a marriage.

The key for everyone to remember is the Lord must give guidance concerning souls in the Church, and the spiritual leader should refrain from involvement unless the Lord tells him to get involved. Hopefully, when the leader does get involved, he will confirm what the Lord instructed the husband. Again, everyone involved must submit to the Lord Jesus. It is also crucial for believers to have the indwelling of the Holy Ghost. Each believer must hear the Lord's voice for themselves; otherwise, confusion will abound. Romans 8:9 informs of the necessity of each believer having the Holy Ghost. *"But ye are not in the flesh, but in the Spirit, if so be that the Spirit of God dwell in you. Now if any man have not the Spirit of Christ, he is none of his."* If the Holy Ghost is not dwelling in you where you can hear His voice daily, then you need to check whether you belong to the Lord. I must say that because many people claim to be Christians. However, they do not know if they belong to the Lord Jesus. That is, according to King James Version Bible Scripture. For that reason, Apostle Peter declared in Acts 2:38, *"Then Peter said unto them, Repent, and be baptized every one of you in the name of Jesus Christ for the remission of sins, and ye shall receive the gift of the Holy Ghost."*

Apostle John also declared, *"Even the Spirit of truth; whom the world cannot receive, because it seeth him not, neither knoweth him: but ye know him; for he dwelleth with you, and shall be in you"* (14:17). If you go to Church and do not have the Holy Ghost, that is partly the problem in your marriage. Please understand that attending a Church does not make a person saved. You must have the Spirit of God abiding in you to belong to Christ. If any party involved in the situation cannot hear from God, it will be impossible for them to agree with the things of God. *"But the natural man receiveth not the things of the Spirit of God: for they are foolishness unto him: neither can he know them, because they are spiritually discerned"* (1st Corinthians 2:14).

Husbands, you need to understand it is not your duty to give your wife everything she desires when she desires it. But the Lord will grant her the desires of her heart when she submits to you. Only then will the Lord move on her behalf. The Bible admonishes husbands to love, nourish, and cherish their wives continually. Love in Ephesians 5:24-33 means you are to be friendly and affectionate with your wife. To nourish her is to build her up and cause her to grow (rear up). When a husband cherishes his wife, he considers her well-being (broods) and promotes her development and growth into a full-bodied woman (fosters). As one can see, the Word of God is not a source of conflict in the marriage. For husbands and wives are called to peace.

On another side, when individuals do not have the Holy Ghost, there will be conflict and confusion with no straightforward remedy in sight. That is why many marriages end in divorce. It is their way of resolving problems. There will also be conflict when there is a lack of teaching and understanding of the Lord's will. Husbands are accountable for teaching their wives, so they will know what the Lord requires of them. Churches are also responsible for teaching husbands and wives to understand what the Lord expects of the couple. There are too many marriages in the Church that have failed because someone gave unscriptural counsel to the couple, mainly the wife. Many Churches also neglect to counsel the husband. Unfortunately, many marriages fail because the couple did not heed the Lord's counsel to stay together. When the Lord says it is His will for you to stay together, stay together!

That is why I believe there are not many men in the Church because they refuse to allow the Lord to lead. They find it difficult to give up control of their lives to the Lord. Matthew 18:3 cautions, *"And said, Verily I say unto you, Except ye be converted, and become as little children, ye shall not enter into the kingdom of heaven."* Husbands are to follow Jesus. He is the only one who knows the marriage's purpose. Can you imagine the Lord instructing a husband

173

to leave a Church, and the Church leader tells the wife not to go, and she stays, yet the husband leaves? That is what displeases the Lord. Have you noticed the number of family members that go to Church by themselves? Unity in the Church starts with harmony in the family. The Lord said of Abraham in Genesis 18:19, *"For I know him, that he will command his children and his household after him, and they shall keep the way of the LORD, to do justice and judgment; that the LORD may bring upon Abraham that which he hath spoken of him."* Husband, your duty is to keep your household on one accord, and only the Lord can help you do that, so let Him lead.

Thirdly, husbands may also feel great anger if they believe the Church is choosing a wife for them and will not allow them to select the woman they truly desire to marry. Consider this scenario: The Lord reveals to a brother in the Church a faithful sister whom he is supposed to marry, but he disagrees with the Lord's decision for his life. However, the man doesn't know the Lord has also shared it with one or more of the Church's spiritual leaders and even told the woman, but no one comes forth and communicates that information. Instead of following the Lord's instruction, the man chooses someone he believes is more suitable and announces his plan to marry his choice. Whether the brother marries according to the Lord's will or

174

not, there will be a great conflict in his heart because his desire and the Lord's plan are not aligned. If he marries the woman he chooses, their marriage will have devastating consequences since he will forfeit the Lord's plan for his life. Suppose he grudgingly marries in the will of God. In that case, he may sabotage the marriage the Lord has chosen for him, not knowing he is hurting himself and simultaneously nullifying the Lord's plan for his life in ministry. His actions also leave the wife the Lord chose in a state of confusion, and she may end up without a covering. She may even abandon the Lord due to mistreatment in the marriage, nullifying the Lord's plan for her life in ministry. Many men and women go back to the world from that type of misunderstanding.

We are counseled by Scripture to continually do the will of God (*"eth"* on the end of any word means continually). Matthew 7:21 declares, *"Not every one that saith unto me, Lord, Lord, shall enter into the kingdom of heaven; but he that doeth the will of my Father which is in heaven."* The Church must teach the importance of doing the will of God, so everyone will desire and pray for His will in their lives. 1st Corinthians 6:19 reminds us, *". . . and ye are not your own?"* We have to make the free-will choice to surrender our lives to the Lord.

Many do not realize marriage is ministry, and ministry is messy, as my husband has taught. Jesus uses the analogy of husband and wife to describe His relationship with the Church. He is the Bridegroom, and the Church is His Bride. Marriage and ministry are no joke. When a man and a woman are in a marriage, they already have a ministry, whether they are believers or not. Marriage and ministry are about serving. In a marriage, you have to serve one another; it's not about sex. It's about humility. In a ministry, you watch for souls. In a marriage, the husband, if he is a believer, watches for the souls of his wife and children. The word Minister means a servant. When someone is married, they have a ministry, and if they are also in ministry over souls, they are responsible for and will give an account for two ministries.

Serving is about sacrificing yourself for someone else. It means unconditional love. If you cannot obey the Lord's instructions on who to marry, then you have no reason to be married. If you refuse to obey the Word of God and apply it to your personal life daily, then you can't watch over souls effectively. A lot of individuals see the platform and desire to be in ministry. Too many long to be on stage in front of the people. However, they do not realize the natural and spiritual implications of being in the pulpit. Nor do people understand the implications of being married. Ministers in various capacities and platforms experience satanic and demonic attacks, and if the spouses are not obedient to the Lord, it will be impossible to withstand the enemy. Believe me. If you are human, you will be attacked by the adversary, mainly because you talk about things you do not understand. Even more so, if you know you have a calling to work for the Lord in any capacity, you will experience intensive attacks by the adversary.

The world teaches to choose a spouse after the flesh, not a Godly spouse. Choosing a spouse after the flesh may mean you make a list and choose someone based on how well they fit your plan. Your list may be a mental picture or a written list of what one believes is the most suitable spouse. Maybe you are looking for someone who looks good physically or has a great family background or someone with a successful career. Perhaps you are looking for someone with complementary skills so you can start a business together. I know a lot of Christian men who are looking for a woman who is sexy and sensual. They do not see the value of marrying someone who is truly the Lord's daughter.

The bottom line is the Lord made Eve for Adam. Adam did not get to choose his wife. It is supposed to mean something special when the Lord chooses a spouse for you. When the Lord joins two together, He has a more excellent plan in mind for both spouses. The Lord's plan exceeds what you can ever imagine. The Lord does not choose a spouse for everyone, yet when He has a more excellent plan in mind, he will determine your spouse, and it is in your best interest to follow His lead.

You must *"die to self"* daily to follow the Lord's plan. Apostle Paul said in 1st Corinthians 15:31, *". . . I die daily."* Husbands and wives need to consistently pray and fast so the Lord can set things in order. The couple should never start blaming the Lord, the Church, or others for their marital problems. Don't even look at each other as the source of the problem. I remind you again of Ephesians 6:12, *"For we wrestle not against flesh and blood, but against principalities, against powers, against the rulers of the darkness of this world, against spiritual wickedness in high places."*

We have to remember we have an adversary, and his job is to bring about confusion to ensure a divisive environment stays in our homes and Churches. A house or Church divided against itself cannot stand (Mark 3:25). Thus, if the adversary can keep the couple at odds, he can keep the house divided. If the adversary can keep the couple in disagreement and strife, he will successfully keep the couple from fulfilling God's will.

Attempts to divide the house include the couple being envious of each other's relationship with the Lord and their status in the Church. Envy leads to strife, then confusion, and then every evil work. *"For where envying and strife is, there is confusion and every evil work,"* James 3:16. False accusations, delusions, and paranoia are the result of an envious heart (character). Envy comes about when a spouse does not know their place in the Lord's grand plan.

Also, keep in mind that many of the feelings some husbands harbor against their wives are not valid. Again, when a husband has negative thoughts and feelings about his wife, the adversary is often the orchestrator. These negative thoughts and feelings will come suddenly and are difficult to resist, causing the husband to believe the thoughts are his own. The Bible declares, *"Husbands, love your wives, and be not bitter against them"* (Colossians 3:19). The enemy enjoys when husbands are bitter against their wives since it opens a door for him to invade the home. When that door opens, all manner of spirits come into the house to cause the children to be restless and idle. Hopelessness plagues everyone in the home to the point where it feels like you exist with no purpose. No one eats together. Everyone is in a rush to live separate lives outside of the family unit. When husbands do not pray, all healthy communication in the home ceases.

In most cases, a husband who is angry with his wife is dissatisfied with his life, and the wife bears the blame for that dissatisfaction. It's worth repeating, *"Likewise, ye husbands, dwell with them according to knowledge, giving honour unto the wife, as unto the weaker vessel, and as being heirs together of the grace of life; that your prayers be not hindered"* (1st Peter 3:7). These Scriptures provide a crucial piece of information about what happens when husbands are unaware of the enemy's tactics and lack the wisdom to keep the household on one accord. Believing husbands must be sober, vigilant, and diligent in their relationship with the Lord so their eyes will be open to see when the enemy is inciting them to hate their wives. They must also know their wives well, so they can dwell with them according to knowledge because they are genuinely the weaker vessel, subject to all manner of spiritual attacks, including mind battles and insecurities. Husbands must present themselves as trustworthy and loyal to their wives, lest she falls through unforgivingness. Women and children need strong God-fearing men to oversee the house, and I'm not talking about a brute or a religious fanatic. Otherwise, the couple will find themselves repeatedly giving the enemy a foothold into their lives. Remember, the Blood of Jesus, coupled with unity, will drive out all the evil spirits fighting against a couple's marriage, especially confusion and discord.

In the Bible, Isaac played, laughed, and was affectionate with his wife, Rebekah. *"And it came to pass, when he had been there a long time, that Abimelech king of the Philistines looked out at a window, and saw, and, behold, Isaac was sporting with Rebekah his wife. And Abimelech called Isaac, and said, Behold, of a surety she is thy wife: and how saidst thou, She is my sister? And Isaac said unto him, Because I said, Lest I die for her"* (Genesis 26:8-9). In that Scripture, Isaac had previously proclaimed to the king that Rebekah was his sister; but, when the king saw them playing together, he knew she was Isaac's wife because of how he sported with her. The king saw how he looked at her and touched her in secret places, like around her waist. That is how my husband is with me. Daily, when I least expect it, he sports with me. It is a powerful tactic to demolish walls of division. It may be difficult for a religious or rigid man to accept, but a willingness to change will bring great satisfaction to the couple and glory to God's Kingdom.

There are too many variables in any given marital situation, and the Lord is the only one who knows the whole truth of a matter,

181

so it is crucial to keep your heart right before the Lord and pray earnestly. Through prayer and fasting, the Lord will correct every situation and all involved as necessary. Don't forget, unity in the home, along with prayer, is the solution.

PRAYING THROUGH A MARITAL CRISIS

As the Lord demonstrated with Job in the Bible, we must go through tests and trials devised by the enemy and approved by the Lord Jesus. However, if we walk in the principles the Lord has laid out for us in Scripture, we will win the battle we face. A marital crisis is one such battle. As couples of all ages and walks of life embark on the first God-given covenant between man and woman, some believe their marriage will be ideal. Others believe in a fairy tale.

In an ideal marriage, the couple will never argue or disagree. The husband will be loving, understanding, and satisfied. The wife will submit to her husband, and neither will ever be discouraged or disappointed. They will never experience failure in any area of their life, and both will always be healthy. They will have the exact number of children they desire when they desire them. The children will be perfectly obedient, and their parents will experience prosperity without loss. They will live an abundant life all of their days. In a fairytale marriage, the couple will experience hardships but will always have a happy ending.

The truth is all marriages will go through difficulties, and a union ordained by the Lord, although prosperous, will experience great sufferings and struggles because the adversary will always seek an occasion to fight against the couple. However, saints do not consider the adversary is behind many problems in their marriage. I remember when my husband and I were going through a great battle in our marriage. Before entering the battle, I saw the adversary standing in our home hallway, leaning on the threshold. It was apparent he had received permission from the Lord to test our marriage. I had already increased my prayer time a couple of months earlier because I knew something was coming, but prayer would not stop the trial. Then midway through the battle, when it looked like the enemy was winning and our house would divide, I saw the adversary in the hallway again leaning on the same threshold.

By that time, more prayer was necessary. I was also anointing myself daily with extra virgin olive oil, which I had prayed over. The Lord kept telling me He was going to increase my prayer time. As my prayer time increased, the Holy Ghost empowered me to be obedient and pray. Now, I was praying up to three hours each day from 2 A.M.

to 5 A.M., walking the floors, and praying in the gift of tongues. Also, I went before the Lord, lying down on my prayer mat in the morning around 8 A.M. to get instructions from the Lord and mid-evening around 8 P.M. to quietly sing worship songs and pray. I was losing weight and sleep. I was not tired when I had to pray because the Holy Ghost anointed me for the task. The battle was intense. I was weak mentally, and I felt sick physically. The trial drained me emotionally. Also, there was unseen pressure to walk away and leave everything and everyone behind.

When you are in a spiritual battle, the enemy will fight your mind by telling you all manner of lies. He will try to make you sick physically, so you can't walk, pray, or fight against him. I felt so ill I lost my appetite, even though I had no sickness in my body. I felt better when I didn't eat, but the Lord told me to make sure I ate regular meals. However, no matter how much I ate, I was still losing weight due to the number of hours I was walking while praying. The battle went on for ten months. I often had uncontrollable crying spells. I was also fighting depression.

I could feel demonic forces fighting against me and would see evil spirits in our home. I continually commanded them to go in the name of Jesus Christ of Nazareth, and the atmosphere would clear up.

184

I could feel the enemy prompting and urging me to give up and to faint, but the Lord kept encouraging me to hold on. The Lord would say, *"I AM with thee. Don't be afraid. Be strong and of good courage. I AM with thee. It's not your battle. It's mine!"* Those words gave me great peace. The Lord also put songs in my spirit throughout the night, so I would be encouraged when I awoke. Those were the songs I listened to throughout the day for added strength.

When you are in a battle with the enemy, his punches and jabs will come by way of mind battles, depression, sickness, physical attacks, weariness, misunderstandings, confusion, strife, fleshly desires, accidents, falls, and more. He will tempt you to fight against the Lord's plan. He will have your flesh fight against you by telling you that you are tired. He will implant thoughts into your mind like, I can't do this anymore. His goal is to cause you to give up fighting for the Lord's will to go forth in your life. But the Bible declares, *"And let us not be weary in well doing: for in due season we shall reap, if we faint not"* (Galatians 6:9).

Moreover, singing spiritual songs, hymns, and thanksgiving to the Lord is an excellent weapon against the enemy (Ephesians 5:19-20). Praise is a garment or a cloak of protection from depression, oppression, sickness, and disease when you are in a battle (Isaiah

61:3). Praise also sets up ambushments against the enemy's attacks (2nd Chronicles 20:22-24). Praise will clear your mind to receive instruction from the Lord.

Once my battle reached its seventh month, the Lord said, *"Give me ninety days."* The last ninety days of the trial were tremendously intensive. Even though the Lord spoke to me about the ninety days, I was still worn and on the brink of giving up. So, I tried to solicit help from other Christians. One person gave me a place of refuge during the day, but I did not ask for prayer, yet they prayed for me anyway. They asked for something specific, and the Lord answered immediately. I only found one other person who prayed for me when I asked, but they were skeptical. No one desired to get involved with my trial, and I didn't blame them. Some also suggested carnal solutions to my spiritual battle. Sometimes it's the Lord's will for you to go through things no one else will understand, nor desire to be of assistance. So expect it to be just you and Jesus. In ninety days, the Lord caused the enemy's plan to fail. He is faithful to do what He says He will do. At the end of the trial, I fell to my knees from exhaustion. I was mentally, emotionally, and physically drained. I rested for months, praying sporadically, and got back on the battlefield.

Matthew 26:38-42 reminds us of Jesus' battle in the Garden of Gethsemane, *"Then saith he unto them, My soul is exceeding sorrowful, even unto death: tarry ye here, and watch with me. And he went a little further, and fell on his face, and prayed, saying, O my Father, if it be possible, let this cup pass from me: nevertheless not as I will, but as thou wilt. And he cometh unto the disciples, and findeth them asleep, and saith unto Peter, What, could ye not watch with me one hour? Watch and pray, that ye enter not into temptation: the spirit indeed is willing, but the flesh is weak. He went away again the second time, and prayed, saying, O my Father, if this cup may not pass away from me, except I drink it, thy will be done."*

Luke's account in 22:39-46 also displays the Lord's agony in the Garden. His disciples were sorrowful too. *"And he came out, and went, as he was wont, to the mount of Olives; and his disciples also followed him. And when he was at the place, he said unto them, Pray that ye enter not into temptation. And he was withdrawn from them about a stone's cast, and kneeled down, and prayed, Saying, Father, if thou be willing, remove this cup from me: nevertheless not my will, but thine, be done. And there appeared an angel unto him from heaven, strengthening him. And being in an agony he prayed more earnestly: and his sweat was as it were great drops of blood falling*

187

down to the ground. And when he rose up from prayer, and was come to his disciples, he found them sleeping for sorrow, And said unto them, Why sleep ye? rise and pray, lest ye enter into temptation." Jesus was in such distress He was weak and *"sweat as it were great drops of blood."* Again, because He spent time praying, He received the strength to pray more earnestly. Prayer helped Him line up with the will of God. It was immediately following His statement to do the will of God that an Angel of the Lord showed up to strengthen Him to finish His mission. However, the disciples did not pray, so they entered into temptation. They all fled after Jesus' arrest, except John. And sadly, Peter got into a violent confrontation and cut off a Centurion's ear. He even denied he knew Jesus. The Lord told them to pray for what was coming, just as I am telling you to pray so you will be spiritually armed and ready for what is coming in your life. If you do not pray, it may be too late to do it once the enemy is upon you.

There is crucial information in these accounts. We see Jesus, while *being in an agony, he prayed more earnestly.* Agony in the Greek (74) means Jesus was in a <u>struggle</u>, that is, He <u>anguished</u>. Jesus also said, *"Why sleep ye? rise and pray, lest ye enter into temptation."* When you are in a spiritual battle, you will have to make sacrifices, just as soldiers do on a physical battlefield. Remember, I said I was losing sleep. I was only resting three hours a day. Think about that for a moment. Naturally, I had little sleep for ten months. Spiritually, I could pray all night long, but my flesh was weak. So weak, I had to push and push my physical body each day to pray. Sadly, many will not pray in situations like this because they do not love enough to make those sacrifices. I know it was the Lord who strengthened me to continue doing His will to pray for my marriage. Only He had the power to strengthen me to the point where the three hours of prayer seemed like five minutes.

Looking back, I understand the battle was so fierce because the house was not on one accord, as we had other people living with us who openly confessed they did not desire to serve the Lord. I was in a delusion, not realizing the seriousness of their open confession. If you have several people in your household who are not aligning their lives with the will of God, it will be challenging to defeat the enemy's attempts to destroy your life. Now, I understand unity in prayer and unity in desiring to do God's will are significant keys in foiling the enemy's plans. Again, Mark 3:25 declares a valuable principle about unity, *"And if a house be divided against itself, that house cannot stand."* Sometimes you can try to help others to your detriment.

Once my husband and I openly expressed our desire to continue to do the will of God, the Lord removed those from our lives who did not desire to serve Him. Sometimes you have to speak that aloud so the enemy will know where you stand. Remember, his goal is to get you to give up. At the end of that spiritual battle, the Lord said to my husband, *"I told the adversary to back off! Way off!"* When I heard that, I remember breathing a great sigh of relief. After all, ultimately, the LORD is in control! *"Ye are of God, little children, and have overcome them: because greater is he that is in you, than he that is in the world"* (1st John 4:4). Whew! *"These things I have spoken unto you, that in me ye might have peace. In the world ye shall have tribulation: but be of good cheer; I have overcome the world"* (John 16:33). Immediately following, we had peace in our home. Peace was the confirmation the adversary was the source of our struggles and troubles. 1st Peter 5:7-9 warns, *"Casting all your care upon him; for he careth for you. Be sober, be vigilant; because your adversary the devil, as a roaring lion, walketh about, seeking whom he may devour: Whom resist stedfast in the faith, knowing that the same afflictions are accomplished in your brethren that are in the world."*

A lot of this is for mature saints. Young saints may feel like they cannot stand in a spiritual battle, although the Word of God declares in Philippians 4:13, *I can do all things through Christ which strengtheneth me.* 2nd Corinthians 12:9 also reveals that the power of God manifests when we feel inadequate and weak. Humility is a key weapon against the enemy. In humility the Lord will move on your behalf. *"And he said unto me, My grace is sufficient for thee: for my strength is made perfect in weakness. Most gladly therefore will I rather glory in my infirmities, that the power of Christ may rest upon me."* Remember these key areas when you are in a spiritual battle for your marriage:

1. Be led by the Holy Ghost in everything you do. *"For as many as are led by the Spirit of God, they are the sons of God"* (Romans 8:14).

2. Inquire of the Lord what you should wear daily, including in what style to wear your hair. It will be a sign of encouragement to you in many ways. You'll see. You also could be wearing the answer to someone's fleece. *"And Gideon said unto God, If thou wilt save Israel by mine hand, as thou hast said, Behold, I will put a fleece of wool in the floor; and if the dew be on the fleece only, and it be*

191

dry upon all the earth beside, then shall I know that thou wilt save Israel by mine hand, as thou hast said. And it was so: for he rose up early on the morrow, and thrust the fleece together, and wringed the dew out of the fleece, a bowl full of water. And Gideon said unto God, Let not thine anger be hot against me, and I will speak but this once: let me prove, I pray thee, but this once with the fleece; let it now be dry only upon the fleece, and upon all the ground let there be dew. And God did so that night: for it was dry upon the fleece only, and there was dew on all the ground" (Judges 6:36-40).

3. Pray for at least one hour a day. If the Holy Ghost increases the time, follow His lead. *"And he cometh unto the disciples, and findeth them asleep, and saith unto Peter, What, could ye not watch with me one hour? Watch and pray, that ye enter not into temptation: the spirit indeed is willing, but the flesh is weak"* (Matthew 26:40-41). As you pray, ask the Holy Ghost to strengthen you to pray the length of time necessary for the season. No matter how difficult, always pray the Lord's will be done. The Lord only grants prayers that align with His will. If you

knowingly press Him for your will to prosper, He may permit your request to your detriment. Please understand, to pray anything other than His will is praying amiss; in essence, you are asking the Lord to give you over to your desires, and that is never good (Proverbs 14:12, 16:25, and 14:14).

4. Keep the household on one accord in everything. *"And Jesus knew their thoughts, and said unto them, Every kingdom divided against itself is brought to desolation; and every city or house divided against itself shall not stand:"* (Matthew 12:25). Agree even in simple things like what meals the family eats. *"IF there be therefore any consolation in Christ, if any comfort of love, if any fellowship of the Spirit, if any bowels and mercies, Fulfil ye my joy, that ye be likeminded, having the same love, being of one accord, of one mind. Let nothing be done through strife or vainglory; but in lowliness of mind let each esteem other better than themselves"* (Philippians 2:1-3).

5. Read the Bible every day and walk in what you read. *"This book of the law shall not depart out of thy mouth;*

but thou shalt meditate therein day and night, that thou mayest observe to do according to all that is written therein: for then thou shalt make thy way prosperous, and then thou shalt have good success. Have not I commanded thee? Be strong and of a good courage; be not afraid, neither be thou dismayed: for the LORD thy God is with thee whithersoever thou goest" (Joshua 1:8-9).

6. Obey all the Lord's instructions. *"If ye love me, keep my commandments. And I will pray the Father, and he shall give you another Comforter, that he may abide with you for ever; Even the Spirit of truth; whom the world cannot receive, because it seeth him not, neither knoweth him: but ye know him; for he dwelleth with you, and shall be in you. I will not leave you comfortless: I will come to you. Yet a little while, and the world seeth me no more; but ye see me: because I live, ye shall live also. At that day ye shall know that I am in my Father, and ye in me, and I in you. He that hath my commandments, and keepeth them, he it is that loveth me: and he that loveth me shall be loved of my Father, and I will love him, and will manifest myself to him. Judas saith unto him, not Iscariot, Lord, how is it that*

194

thou wilt manifest thyself unto us, and not unto the world?

Jesus answered and said unto him, If a man love me, he

will keep my words: and my Father will love him, and we

will come unto him, and make our abode with him. He that

loveth me not keepeth not my sayings: and the word which

ye hear is not mine, but the Father's which sent me. These

things have I spoken unto you, being yet present with you.

But the Comforter, which is the Holy Ghost, whom the

Father will send in my name, he shall teach you all things,

and bring all things to your remembrance, whatsoever I

have said unto you. Peace I leave with you, my peace I

give unto you: not as the world giveth, give I unto you. Let

not your heart be troubled, neither let it be afraid. Ye have

heard how I said unto you, I go away, and come again

unto you. If ye loved me, ye would rejoice, because I said,

I go unto the Father: for my Father is greater than I. And

now I have told you before it come to pass, that, when it is

come to pass, ye might believe. Hereafter I will not talk

much with you: for the prince of this world cometh, and

hath nothing in me. But that the world may know that I

love   the   Father;   and   as   the   Father   gave   me commandment, even so I do. Arise, let us go hence" (John 14:15-31).

7. Remember, the angels of the Lord are the ones engaging in the fight. As you pray, the Holy angels fight and defeat the evil forces assigned to destroy the Lord's purpose for you and your family (Daniel 10:1-21).

8. Just because you cannot stop Satan's attack, it does not mean you will not foil his plan. The Lord said, *"No weapon that is formed against thee shall prosper; and every tongue that shall rise against thee in judgment thou shalt condemn. This is the heritage of the servants of the LORD, and their righteousness is of me, saith the LORD"* (Isaiah 54:17). The Scripture strongly indicates that the enemy will devise a weapon, whether he uses an evil spirit, person, or vice. Thankfully, no one knows the outcome except the Lord. If you choose to fight, the outcome will end in your favor (Romans 8:28). If you do not fight, you will lose everything, even your soul. Keep in mind the enemy is always coming for your soul. When he attacked Job, the point was to get Job to curse God (Job

1:11). If Job had cursed God, he would have died and perished (Job 2:9).

9. Never forget the battle is not yours. It's the Lord's. You are more than a conqueror through Christ Jesus (Romans 8:37).

10. As you obey the Lord, expect Him to reveal the whole truth to you. One morning, the Lord woke me up at 2 A.M. I went to my prayer closet to lie on my prayer mat. As I was praying and worshipping quietly, Jesus came into my closet; His presence was likened unto a thick cloud. I mean, it was weighty. He told me all the details of my battle. He talked with me for three hours. I wrote what He said and told my husband, who expounded on what the Lord was saying. Although we were armed with knowledge, the battle did not get easier but grew worse. So, I fought harder. Then the Lord gave me a strategy that knocked my enemies off of their feet. Love was the foundation of the Lord's plan. Yep! Love helped destroy what the adversary was trying to do. When the response is love, the enemy can't stand. *"And above all things have*

fervent charity [love] *among yourselves: for charity* [love]

shall cover the multitude of sins" (1st Peter 4:8).

SOMETHING TO CONSIDER

Finally, have you ever seen a glimpse of what your life would be like if you were not in the will of the Lord? I have. I genuinely believe you would be more apt to forgive those who hurt you if you could see a glimpse of what your life will become if you do not let go of Church hurt. It would change your mindset if you saw yourself in Hell because you didn't forgive. It would change your life if you caught a glimpse of what it would be like to experience eternal damnation because you left the will of God. You would decide to live for Jesus if you saw yourself lonely and miserable for the rest of your natural life because you refused to endure the will of God or His planned season of suffering for your life.

You would have a new heart if you could see how things would turn out because you did not take up your cross to follow the Lord Jesus. Taking up your cross means you have a resolve to do whatever the Lord Jesus requires of you. It implies you obey the Lord in everything. Your cross is tailor-made for you. That means He may instruct you to quit your job, release family members, friends, marry a

198

particular person, abandon your plans for schooling, stay employed at a certain place, live in a specific home, specified city, or country. Your cross usually includes the things that you would choose instead of eternal life.

I believe if you saw a glimpse of your future, you would not allow your thoughts to counsel you to leave or sabotage your marriage. You would be less inclined to leave your spouse or leave the Church, and you definitely would not hate on people. If you had a foretaste of your life, you would not blame other people or the Church for your problems. You would do things differently if you could just see what your life will be like if you marry the wrong person. You would have a change of heart, mind, and attitude toward the Lord and the Church. If you could see the horrors you will bring upon your soul, you would go through that test and trial and would never give up. You would readily endure whatever the Lord desired to put you through if you saw the depth of darkness you would descend to for abandoning the will of God.

Too many have ruined their lives because they lacked an understanding of why it is crucial to complete God's will. Too many have missed the move of God because they fulfilled their desires. I beg you: Strive to fulfill the will of God! Remember, it pleased the

Father to beat to pieces, humble, oppress, crush and smite Jesus Christ, His only Begotten Son. How much more will *He* allow to be done to those who hope to reign with Christ? *"Yet it pleased the LORD to bruise him; he hath put him to grief: when thou shalt make his soul an offering for sin, he shall see his seed, he shall prolong his days, and the pleasure of the LORD shall prosper in his hand"* (Isaiah 53:10). Yeah. The glimpses He has given me throughout my life helped me tremendously. They have urged me to continue in the Lord, and *"I press toward the mark for the prize of the high calling of God in Christ Jesus. Let us therefore, as many as be perfect, be thus minded: and if in any thing ye be otherwise minded, God shall reveal even this unto you"* (Philippians 3:14-15).

Reader, pray these prayers with me:

Prayer of repentance: Abba, Father, in the name of Jesus Christ of Nazareth, I recognize I am a sinner, and I believe You sent Your Son Jesus Christ that I might have forgiveness for my sins. I repent for my sins, and I confess the Lord Jesus with my mouth. I believe in my heart that Jesus Christ died for my sins, and God raised him from the dead. Please grant me the indwelling of the Holy Spirit with the gift of tongues. Write my name in the *Lamb's Book of Life* and send me to the Church You would have me attend so I may be in Your perfect and divine will. I need a Church home so I can grow in You and fellowship with the saints. In Jesus' name. Amen.

Prayer for the marriage: Abba, Father, in the name of Jesus Christ of Nazareth, I know You are in control of all things. I pray You will lead and guide my spouse and me concerning how You would have our marriage operate. Please align all things in our lives with Your plan. Align our marriage with the Word of God and get the glory out of our lives in Jesus' name. Abba, Father, I break every ungodly bond that is fighting against our marriage. Lord, I pray You will not allow the evil devices of the enemy to prosper against my marriage, in Jesus' name. Lord, break every yoke of the enemy in

Jesus' name. Break every chain in the name of Jesus. Strengthen us to pray as a family. Teach us to successfully war against the enemy's plan to destroy our marriage in Jesus' name. Amen.

Prayer to do the will of God: Abba, Father, in the name of Jesus Christ of Nazareth, teach me to do Thy will and perfect those things that concern my family and me. Remove the blindness from our minds and the scales from our eyes so that we can see Your plan for our lives. Empower us to walk in the newness of life through Jesus Christ, in Jesus' name. Amen.

CHAPTER NINE

DID YOU DO IT FOR ME? saith the LORD!

"But ye, brethren, be not weary in well doing."

2nd *Thessalonians 3:13*

CHAPTER 9: *DID YOU DO IT FOR ME? saith the LORD!*

Colossians 3:23-24 declares, *"And whatsoever ye do, do it heartily, as to the Lord, and not unto men; Knowing that of the Lord ye shall receive the reward of the inheritance: for ye serve the Lord Christ."* Are you hurt because a Church offended you by not acknowledging the work you did? Are you angry because they did not recognize the physical and spiritual labor you exerted to build a ministry? Did your financial investments in the Church go unnoticed? Did the Church lack to appreciate the prayers you laid down for the saints? Did the saints forget to show gratitude when you volunteered to transport souls to and from the Church? Did someone despise the personal and familial sacrifices you made for the Church? Did you do something for the Church, and the saints neglected to say, "Thank you?" If you replied yes to any of those questions, this chapter is for you.

Another form of Church hurt is when spiritual leaders do not recognize your labor in the Lord's Kingdom. Especially if you were there faithfully serving from the beginning. Ah! You delighted in and felt special doing the work of the Lord. You felt the Lord needed you and had a plan to utilize your skills and anointing. As long as others depended on you, there was a connection to the Church. However, let me ask you a question: Did you do it for the Lord Jesus or man? If you are hurting for not being acknowledged after all your hard work and sacrifices, you did not do it for the Lord. You did it to please humans.

The problem with feeling favored in the Church is complicated because people will change. The Lord may change a Ministry's mission or structure. Maybe you fulfilled your service. The Lord often sends new saints to a Ministry who are more qualified or anointed for a particular task. Frankly, Jesus may be calling you to do something different, something that exceeds what you are currently doing. However, when we are shortsighted and can only see ourselves in our present state, doing what we have always been doing for the rest of our lives, we are then in a place where Jesus will try all we are doing and why we are doing it. We should be moving with the cloud.

1st Corinthians 1:25-31 helps us understand, *"Because the foolishness of God is wiser than men; and the weakness of God is stronger than men. For ye see your calling, brethren, how that not many wise men after the flesh, not many mighty, not many noble, are called: But God hath chosen the foolish things of the world to confound the wise; and God hath chosen the weak things of the world to confound the things which are mighty; And base things of the world, and things which are despised, hath God chosen, yea, and things which are not, to bring to nought things that are: That no flesh should glory in his presence. But of him are ye in Christ Jesus, who of God is made unto us wisdom, and righteousness, and sanctification, and redemption: That, according as it is written, He that glorieth, let him glory in the Lord."* Church leaders understand we are to glory in the Lord and not those who labor in the Church. Once we start giving accolades, everyone in the Church will require praise. Jesus is the only one who should be lifted and praised.

I am not telling you to eliminate saying thank you; as a child, I learned to say thank you, and you're welcome. What I am saying is those who feel they deserve a thank you have the wrong mindset. I have experienced people going overboard with acknowledgments and accolades. Some of it was not even sincere, and some favorable remarks were just false. Those false compliments were all about a human trying to glorify another human. I understand the need for people to feel important, but sometimes it is overrated. If I have to stroke your ego to keep you returning to Church or keep you smiling, you are not in service to the Lord. You desire to put on a show. When a person truly understands the sacrifice Jesus made for them on the cross, they are willing to sacrifice everything for Him, and no one has to tell that person thank you.

Christians have come to me and said, thank you for praying for me. Okay, I prayed for you. Now, think about it: Aren't you praying for me? Aren't all the saints supposed to be praying for one another? It is a part of our reasonable service, right? If it is a part of our reasonable service to the Lord, then why do we feel the need to tell one person in the Church, "Thank you for praying for me?" Who gave them the heart to pray for you? Who woke them up in the midnight hour to pray for you? I'm trying to make a point. Who gave them the strength to pray for you? Who empowered them to pray? Who gave them the authority to pray? I'm trying to make a point.

Are they able to answer the prayers? Are they pleading on your behalf, or is it Jesus Christ the hope of glory in them praying for you by the Holy Ghost? Saints don't know what to pray for or how to pray. It is the Holy Ghost doing the praying according to the will of God. Romans 8:26-27 declares, *"Likewise the Spirit also helpeth our infirmities: for we know not what we should pray for as we ought: but the Spirit itself maketh intercession for us with groanings which cannot be uttered. And he that searcheth the hearts knoweth what is the mind of the Spirit, because he maketh intercession for the saints according to the will of God."* When you see the word Spirit capitalized in the Bible, it means the Holy Spirit. It is the Holy Ghost praying. Give glory to the Lord and not man!

There are too many saints expecting honor and glory. That's when we run into problems. If you assume the saints owe you something, then your heart is not in the right place. The Word of God declares in Romans 13:8, *"Owe no man any thing, but to love one another: for he that loveth another hath fulfilled the law."* Listen, there were times when special occasions came up in the Church, and those occasions usually warranted a celebration for me. However, there was no celebration. That happened to me more than once. So what was I to do? Get angry and say I'm leaving this Church because you all forgot about me? What would you do? Would you repay the deed and forget others when it is time for their celebration? Would you start dishonoring others? Remember, don't render evil for evil (1st Peter 3:9). The Lord God remembers you and your labor. Let Him reward you. Besides, if you get all your rewards while you are on Earth, will you receive any heavenly rewards (Matthew 5:11-12)? Only the Lord knows. Jesus warned us in Matthew 6:1, *"TAKE heed that ye do not your alms before men, to be seen of them: otherwise ye have no reward of your Father which is in heaven."*

There will be times in your life when you will need a memorial offering for the Lord. Your labor toward His Kingdom is just the offering you need. 2nd Kings 4:1-7 declares, *"NOW there cried a certain woman of the wives of the sons of the prophets unto Elisha, saying, Thy servant my husband is dead; and thou knowest that thy servant did fear the LORD: and the creditor is come to take unto him my two sons to be bondmen. And Elisha said unto her, What shall I do for thee? tell me, what hast thou in the house? And she said, Thine handmaid hath not any thing in the house, save a pot of oil. Then he said, Go, borrow thee vessels abroad of all thy neighbours, even empty vessels; borrow not a few. And when thou art come in, thou shalt shut the door upon thee and upon thy sons, and shalt pour out into all those vessels, and thou shalt set aside that which is full. So she went from him, and shut the door upon her and upon her sons, who brought the vessels to her; and she poured out. And it came to pass, when the vessels were full, that she said unto her son, Bring me yet a vessel. And he said unto her, There is not a vessel more. And the oil stayed. Then she came and told the man of God. And he said, Go, sell the oil, and pay thy debt, and live thou and thy children of the rest."* That is a prime example of someone laboring faithfully in the house of God and the Lord rewarding them for their works of service.

Elisha's servant was the beneficiary, even though the blessing fell to his wife and sons. Talk about an instant business with debt-free inventory.

There are many reasons the Lord will not give honor to someone. If honoring that person will cause them to walk in pride, He will not have them honored. Just do what you do as unto the Lord. I know the Scriptures about giving honor where honor is due (Romans 13:7) and giving double honor to the Elders who rule well (1st Timothy 5:17). If being honored is so vital to you that the last two Scriptures came to mind as you read this chapter, your heart is not in the right place. Please check the condition of your heart. If your heart is not in the right place, it will be a source of pain. Imagine your physical heart being out of place. Boy! It would hurt and make you sick! It would hurt if your heart were on the outside of your chest (ectopia cordis) or if it pointed in the wrong direction (dextrocardia). Jeremiah 17:10 is a great truth, *"I the LORD search the heart, I try the reins, even to give every man according to his ways, and according to the fruit of his doings."*

Another thing that complicates serving in the Church is when someone has made significant contributions and tends to feel no one can correct them or question what they do. One can feel privileged

211

and influential when contributing to so many areas of the Church. Congregants depend too much on their leaders. But the leader is not the Lord. Jesus desires to have a personal relationship with you. Too often, leaders are put on pedestals and labeled faultless. Then people start to see them as idols. You will know you worship your leader when the Lord sends other men and women of God to give you a message, but you will not listen to the Lord through them. Unfortunately, when congregants worship their leaders, it will kindle the Lord's righteous jealousy, and the leader will be exposed to be human. I have seen leaders fall because the congregation overemphasized the leader's non-scriptural teachings. For example, some leaders teach their Church members not to listen to the Lord in other people. When I was a layperson, the Lord used sinner and saint alike to speak His truths to me. Each time I knew it was the Lord. Too many believers praise the leader for what the Lord is doing in the lives of His children.

Nevertheless, the spotlight needs to be on Jesus. The Lord will not share His glory, and rightfully so, because He is the one who died for the whole world. I know the Lord will use humans to bless His Kingdom, yet the Lord is the one anointing and empowering the leaders and the brethren to do all they do. We are foolish when we take credit for what the Lord is doing! *"For in him we live, and move, and have our being; . . . For we are also his offspring"* (Acts 17:28). What if you outlive the leader you are worshipping? What will you do then? None of us can do anything without the Lord, so why are humans getting all the glory? Churches experience stagnation when there is too much emphasis on humans and not Jesus. Those who are sincere do not go to Church to be entertained by the flesh. They are coming because they need a touch from Jesus!

When someone is influential and vital to a Church, it may cause friction if the person of influence is not humble. For that reason, you must humble yourself. If you do not, the Lord will have to humiliate you. In my experience, the Lord will allow people in the Church to do things to you. It's the baptism of fire, which comes to try every man's work. If you are truly doing all you do for Jesus, there will come a time when you will suffer things at the hand of man. If you humble yourself, you will be able to get through it, and it will build your character. But if you are prideful, it will be a long hard road, and you will probably run, only to find the test waiting on you somewhere else.

Again, the Lord will allow people in the Church to challenge you with specific things as a way of trying you. Perhaps it is appointed for you to suffer humiliation in front of the congregation, like falling off the choir stand or tripping while walking down the aisle. Maybe the leader eliminated your position. It may be your lot to be escorted out of the Church like a criminal and told never to return. Perhaps the Lord will allow an accusation to come forth concerning you doing some evil in the Church (true or false). Peradventure, the Lord will have someone correct you openly in front of the congregation. However, being scorned by the brethren will not have long-term effects or cause you extreme pain if your heart is in the right place in the Lord. That is, it will not hurt if you are laboring sincerely, not desiring to be seen, and not caring one bit what humans think about you. I know what I am talking about since I have had many of these things happen to me. Yet, I looked to the hills from whence cometh my help and kept my eyes, and my heart fixed on Jesus, knowing I shall receive a reward from Him.

I used to do women's meetings regularly. Then the Lord told me to tell the women He would stop the meetings because they did not follow the teachings. One month later, Jesus told me to minister something specific at a women's meeting. I did everything He told me to do, and there was a backlash from some women. The next day I experienced reproof in front of the congregation, and future meetings

214

were canceled. Afterward, I was in my prayer closet, sniveling, saying, Lord, I did everything you told me to do. What happened? He responded, *"I never said it would turn out well."* Wow! I had to change my mindset because I mistakenly thought if I did everything the Lord told me to do that day, all the women would leave excited and blessed with understanding. That was not the case, yet it was good for it to happen because I learned a valuable lesson. I remembered Jesus did everything God the Father told Him to do, and they crucified Him. He was humiliated in front of the world, and that story is still told today. Thank the LORD! Serving the Lord and being obedient to Him does not relieve you of suffering at the hands of man.

When the Lord appoints you a season of suffering, you will not only find out where the hearts of others are toward you, but more importantly, you will find out where your heart is toward the Lord and the brethren. If you can no longer sit in the chief seat, whether by God or man, sit in the back, and don't expect the Lord to exalt you later. Don't expect anything. Abase yourself because you desire people to see Jesus and not you. No one can receive salvation if they are looking at you. People are hurting and need Jesus. If you are the center of attention, then you are not exalting the Lord Jesus. John 12:32 declares, *"And I, if I be lifted up from the earth, will draw all men unto me."* Jesus is the only one who died for humanity, and He will not give His glory to another nor allow anyone to glory in His presence (1st Corinthians 1:29). So, looking for acknowledgment is a quick way to get into trouble with the Lord. And frankly, it is a form of idolatry with you being the idol. Isaiah 42:8 declares, *"I am the LORD: that is my name: and my glory will I not give to another, neither my praise to graven images."*

You don't need anyone praising you for the thing the Lord gave you the skill or money to do. It is not you who've accomplished all the things you have accomplished, but the Lord in you. Many in the Church say, "It's not about me; it's about Jesus." Yet, they are always promoting themselves. Moreover, when it's time to give the Lord glory, proving Jesus is Lord and acknowledging the reason we are all in the Church, they say someone hurt them by not recognizing all they did for Jesus and the Church. 2nd Corinthians 10:17-18 declares, *"But he that glorieth, let him glory in the Lord. For not he that commendeth himself is approved, but whom the Lord commendeth."*

Plus, sometimes someone will say to you, "Don't you regret giving all that money to the Church? Don't you regret all the Saturdays you spent painting the Church building? Aren't you the one who did this or that? See, they didn't even acknowledge you." 1ˢᵗ Corinthians 3:9-15 declares, *"For we are labourers together with God: ye are God's husbandry, ye are God's building. According to the grace of God which is given unto me, as a wise master builder, I have laid the foundation, and another buildeth thereon. But let every man take heed how he buildeth thereupon. For other foundation can no man lay than that is laid, which is Jesus Christ. Now if any man build upon this foundation gold, silver, precious stones, wood, hay, stubble; Every man's work shall be made manifest: for the day shall declare it, because it shall be revealed by fire; and the fire shall try every man's work of what sort it is. If any man's work abide which he hath built thereupon, he shall receive a reward. If any man's work shall be burned, he shall suffer loss: but he himself shall be saved; yet so as by fire."*

A lack of recognition in the Church is a blow to the ego and comes about through misplaced loyalties. Misplaced loyalties come in many forms. However, in each case, heartache is sure to follow. Let me explain. Throughout the previous chapters, I talked about some of the ways people have hurt other people. As humans, we open the door for hurts and pains because we emphasize other people reciprocating love. That is a form of misplaced loyalties. Not only do we have a

217

misconception of love, but we also place our trust in people and things as if life will stay the same from day to day and never change. The truth is people and situations are changing all around us every day. If we had our loyalties in the right place, we would not be surprised when the Lord sends adversity.

Thankfully, our existence has many facets. Our lifestyles consist of all the things necessary for us to survive and thrive daily, but everyday living also has downsides. Some of the disappointments in life include marriages ending in divorce, sterility, the barrenness of the womb, unemployment, failed businesses, and crushed dreams. For some, life has too much heartache to mention. Unfortunately, life is unpredictable.

Churches will change locations, and leaders will change positions. Church visions and missions will evolve. And the Lord will move his children from one vineyard to another. The Lord even drives people out of Churches when they refuse to line up with his will. I know all these things may be hurtful. However, we often see these occurrences as so detrimental that we cannot go on because of misplaced loyalties. Many people see change as a negative thing and find it difficult to cope, inviting a spirit of depression, causing the one hurting to become unfruitful. But, we need to be adaptable to follow the Lord because He will continually work to reshape our character. *"TO every thing there is a season, and a time to every purpose under the heaven:"* (Ecclesiastes 3:1).

When the Lord Jesus was in His incarnate nature, He taught us a valuable lesson about loyalties. He was only loyal to God the Father in Heaven because, after all, the Father is the only one who is immutable and faithful. Remember when Jesus was a young boy, and His family went to Jerusalem to the feast of the Passover, and Jesus disappeared, and the family searched for Him? Well, recall what happened when they found Him in the temple doing His Father's will. Jesus said unto them in Luke 2:49, *". . . How is it that ye sought me? wist ye not that I must be about my Father's business?"* That's hard, but Jesus had a mission to accomplish.

Remember when Peter urged Jesus not to go to Jerusalem, and the Lord rebuked Satan and said: *". . . for thou savourest not the things that be of God, but those that be of men"* (Matthew 16:23). Satan incited fear in Peter in an attempt to hinder the Lord from doing the Father's will. As much as Jesus loved Peter, He would not allow Peter to hinder Him. Jesus' loyalties were to God the Father only. Remember, in the Garden of Gethsemane, when the men came to arrest Jesus and Peter used his sword to cut off one of the Centurion's ear (Mark 14:47), and Jesus rebuked Peter and healed the servant's ear (Luke 22:49-51)? Jesus said, *". . . Put up again thy sword into his place . . . :"* If I desired to fight and circumvent the will of God, I could pray, and my Father would presently give me more than twelve legions of angels (Matthew 26:51-54).

The point is Jesus did not have divided loyalties. He was not expecting humans to acknowledge Him or pat Him on the back. The Lord Jesus purposed to please God the Father. Jesus committed Himself to no human because He knows what is in humans (John 2:24). Even Apostle Paul declared in Galatians 1:10, *"For do I now persuade men, or God? or do I seek to please men? for if I yet pleased men, I should not be the servant of Christ."* If it were up to men, Paul would not have been serving the Lord, and after persecuting the Church, many thought he was not worthy to preach the Gospel.

With misplaced loyalties, we love conditionally. Conditional love declares: I will love you if you love me. I will treat you well if you treat me well. I will honor my vows if you keep your vows. I will love you if you meet all of my expectations. If you make me happy, then I will love you. If you acknowledge my good deeds toward you, then I will recognize your actions towards me. If you respect me, then

I will respect you. Luke 6:32-36 warns, *"For if ye love them which love you, what thank have ye? for sinners also love those that love them. And if ye do good to them which do good to you, what thank have ye? for sinners also do even the same. And if ye lend to them of whom ye hope to receive, what thank have ye? for sinners also lend to sinners, to receive as much again. But love ye your enemies, and do good, and lend, hoping for nothing again; and your reward shall be great, and ye shall be the children of the Highest: for he is kind unto the unthankful and to the evil. Be ye therefore merciful, as your Father also is merciful."* Misplaced loyalties will have a person thinking everything is about them and how they feel, but we should all be seeking to do the Father's will no matter the cost or the sacrifice. We should all be in the same mindset as Jesus: *"For I came down from heaven, not to do mine own will, but the will of him that sent me"* (John 6:38).

Your healing will come about when you repent for having the wrong heart and mindset concerning laboring in the Church. When you get your loyalties in order, Jesus being in the forefront, your heart and mind will line up with the Lord's will, and you will see Him as the one working in the Body of Christ and not you. The Lord will then liberate you from the need to be important. You will also start to feel abundant peace and joy while working in the house of God and laboring to assist the saints. You will also see the Lord move in your life and on your behalf because you are placing Him first and giving Him all the praise, honor, and glory. 1st Corinthians 15:58 admonishes, *"Therefore, my beloved brethren, be ye steadfast, unmoveable, always abounding in the work of the Lord, forasmuch as ye know that your labour is not in vain in the Lord."*

Reader, pray this prayer with me:

Abba, Father, in the name of Jesus Christ of Nazareth, forgive me for having misplaced loyalties. Forgive me for not seeing the brethren and the Church how You see them. I understand if I'm angry with the Church for not recognizing my labor, then I'm angry with You because You are the only one who can acknowledge my service. Forgive me for not doing all I did as unto You. Work Your will in my life. Do all You have to do so my heart will be in the right place. Do what You have to do to ensure I'm doing what pleases You in this season. I understand what You have planned to correct my character may not feel good, but give me peace and understanding and a desire to cooperate with the Holy Ghost through the process. Let the truth of how I genuinely feel about serving in Your Kingdom be made manifest unto me. Perfect me in this area of my character. Leave no stone unturned, so I will not perish with the world in Jesus' name. Amen!

CHAPTER TEN

FAITH WITHOUT WORKS IS DEAD

"And the Lord said, If ye had faith as a grain of mustard seed, ye might say unto this sycamine tree, Be thou plucked up by the root, and be thou planted in the sea; and it should obey you."

Luke 17:6

"What doth it profit, my brethren, though a man say he hath faith, and have not works? can faith save him? If a brother or sister be naked, and destitute of daily food, And one of you say unto them, Depart in peace, be ye warmed and filled; notwithstanding ye give them not those things which are needful to the body; what doth it profit? Even so faith, if it hath not works, is dead, being alone. Yea, a man may say, Thou hast faith, and I have works: shew me thy faith without thy works, and I will shew thee my faith by my works. Thou believest that there is one God; thou doest well: the devils also believe, and tremble. But wilt thou know, O vain man, that faith without works is dead? Was not Abraham our father justified by works, when he had offered Isaac his son upon the altar? Seest thou how faith wrought with his works, and by works was faith made perfect? And the scripture was fulfilled which saith, Abraham believed God, and it was imputed unto him for righteousness: and he was called the Friend of God. Ye see then how that by works a man is justified, and not by faith only. Likewise also was not Rahab the harlot justified by works, when she had received the messengers, and

had sent them out another way? For as the body without the spirit is dead, so faith without works is dead also" (James 2:14-26).

What unfulfilled dreams and desires do you have? Who are you blaming for your unfulfilled dreams? Today, many in the Church are hurting because they feel they did not live up to their potential or did not experience what the Lord promised He would do in their lives. There are many reasons why the Lord's plan for some areas of your life has not come to pass. It could be you did not prepare for the blessing the Lord had for you, or you were not obedient to the Lord's instructions concerning something specific. It could also be the wrong season. Maybe there are weaknesses in your character that are the hindrance. Preparation, obedience, character, and timing are connected to you obtaining the Lord's promises.

I remember when the Lord said He was going to send me a husband during a particular year. When my espoused husband arrived, the Lord instructed me to make sure I did not say anything about him. Later, I found out my promised husband was Apostolic Prophetic authority. If I would have said something evil about him, how would it have altered the Lord's plan to give me that particular man for a blessing? Why did the Lord have to provide me with specific instructions concerning him? Shortly after the Lord gave me those instructions, someone came to me talking about my future blessing. They did not know he was to be my husband. I knew, but they didn't. I quickly changed the subject because I remembered the Lord's instructions. Complete obedience to the Lord's instructions will usher in your blessings, whereas your disobedience may cause you to suffer loss.

Another reason the Lord's plan may have gone unfulfilled is the Lord planned, from the beginning, to have you wait years on your blessing. Some Prophetic Officers see afar off. So, when they prophesy or the Lord shows you something personally, it pertains to something decades or centuries later. Also, some prophecies to you may be for your posterity. Moreover, you may not have received what the Lord promised you because your heart (character) toward the Lord and His work is just not right. You will hinder your blessings if you always have negative things to say when the Lord requires something of you. You may even forfeit some blessings. Many saints tend to murmur and complain when the Lord reveals His plan for a particular area of their life. And, oftentimes, it is not their words that hinder them. It is their thoughts. If you disagree with whatever the Lord is doing in your life, you are only hindering yourself. Murmuring and complaining never change the will of God, yet these may disqualify you from fulfilling His will. In that case, it will likely pass to your children or die with you. Why would that be? Because you refuse to stop murmuring and complaining. You refuse to line up with the will of God.

Gossip is another hindrance. *"And the great dragon was cast out, that old serpent, called the Devil, and Satan, which deceiveth the whole world: he was cast out into the earth, and his angels were cast out with him. And I heard a loud voice saying in heaven, Now is come salvation, and strength, and the kingdom of our God, and the power of his Christ: for the accuser of our brethren is cast down, which accused them before our God day and night. And they overcame him by the blood of the Lamb, and by the word of their testimony; and they loved not their lives unto the death"* (Revelation 12:9-11).

The Bible declares Satan is the accuser of the brethren. If you are a gossiper, you are working for the devil. If you are gossiping about the Lord's children or have your mouth on His spiritual leaders, then you are doing all manner of damage to the Kingdom of God. If you are a gossiper, then you are hindering souls and making yourself an enemy of God. Jesus said, *"He that is not with me is against me; and he that gathereth not with me scattereth abroad"* Matthew 12:30. If you are an enemy of the Lord, you will not receive anything the

Lord promised you. Instead, He will turn and do you great hurt. *"If ye forsake the LORD, and serve strange gods, then he will turn and do you hurt, and consume you, after that he hath done you good"* (Joshua 24:20). If you work for the devil, you are serving a strange god.

Is all lost for someone who has done extensive damage to the Kingdom of Heaven? I don't know. What I do know is Saul of Tarsus did considerable damage to the early Church, and he obtained mercy. But he had to repent. *"But the Lord said unto him, Go thy way: for he is a chosen vessel unto me, to bear my name before the Gentiles, and kings, and the children of Israel: For I will shew him how great things he must suffer for my name's sake"* (Acts 9:15-16). If you genuinely repent, the Lord will grant you mercy. However, the Lord's original intent for your life may change, and you will suffer the consequences of hindering the work of the Lord. After the Lord has forgiven you, follow the instructions given in 1st Peter 3:10-12, *"For he that will love life, and see good days, let him refrain his tongue from evil, and his lips that they speak no guile: Let him eschew evil, and do good; let him seek peace, and ensue it. For the eyes of the Lord are over the righteous, and his ears are open unto their prayers: but the face of the Lord is against them that do evil."*

Lackadaisical behavior is another reason you may not have received specific blessings. Most believers do not realize that they have to do their part to accomplish what the Lord promised them. Sometimes it is working in His house, surrendering offerings, and praying. Some things naturally need to be done to accomplish the Lord's will. If you do not put anything in, you will get nothing out. The Lord makes a promise and empowers us to fulfill His plan for our lives, yet we are the ones who run with the vision. *"And the LORD answered me, and said, Write the vision, and make it plain upon tables, that he may run that readeth it"* (Habakkuk 2:2). When the Lord promises you something, He equips you to accomplish it.

Unfortunately, too many believers today hear the Word of the Lord and just sit idle and wait for it to come to pass. I, also, have been guilty of letting the promises of the Lord slip away while I wait on God. The truth is He was waiting for me. What was He waiting for me to do? The Lord was waiting for me to walk in righteousness and use the gifts and talents He gave me. If the Lord says to write a book, just start writing, asking the Lord what to write every step of the way. Don't ever think, for any reason, that you cannot do what the Lord says you will do. If the Lord told you to do it, just write the book. Once you are obedient, the Lord will open the doors He plans to open.

When we first started the ministry, I had an opportunity to use the Psalmist anointing the Lord gave me. In that season, the Lord began giving me psalms and hymns to be a blessing to the house of God. Two years prior, the Lord had a Prophetess tell me, *"He would give me songs that would deliver my house."* I wrestled with others to develop my gift because some in the congregation always complained when I came forth with new songs. They said, "I can't hit that note. Can I sing it like this instead? Why is it written like that? That verse should go here or there!" So I started singing some of the songs I wrote without letting the congregation know I was the songwriter. As long as they were unaware that I was the songwriter, they liked the songs.

I kept writing and singing the songs in my own devotion time but did not sing many of them at Church, which hindered me much. My husband, the Man of God over the ministry, kept telling me to sing the songs I wrote in Church. I did, but not consistently. You see, the Lord never said to me, daughter, some will oppose you, but don't be afraid, I AM with thee, keep songwriting and singing. No, He didn't say anything because I should have known already I would face opposition. Now, after many years, I have more than a hundred songs. Lately, the Lord has been saying to me, *"You will record this* song." Guess what? I have to get busy doing what is necessary to record the song. And get this, the Lord said I could not go the traditional route because they will exploit me. He knows I desire to stay saved. Understand, I have not had professional training, and I'm expected to record songs.

When the Lord called you, He knew all about you and your struggles. He knew your shortcomings and still chose you. He also endowed you with everything you needed to be successful in Him. Moses, the servant of the Lord, was equipped with a rod. A rod! That's it! What if Moses told the Lord, where is my armor? Where is my sword? Don't I get a chariot and horses? Where is my army? I'll need at least 100,000 men to go into battle with me. After all, Lord, I'm going to war with Pharaoh, king of Egypt. Okay, Lord, since You haven't given me everything I need to battle against Pharaoh, I guess I will not be going to battle.

Once Moses came to terms with what the Lord had chosen him to do, he understood all he needed was that rod and the power of God to accomplish Israel's deliverance. *"And the LORD said unto Moses, Wherefore criest thou unto me? speak unto the children of Israel, that they go forward: But lift thou up thy rod, and stretch out thine hand over the sea, and divide it: and the children of Israel shall*

234

go on dry ground through the midst of the sea" (Exodus 14:15-16). Moses did not have to be a great orator or have a mighty army. The only thing the children of Israel needed was faith and courage to get up and leave Egypt. The Lord God fought for Israel like He has no other nation since. All they had to do was put their hands to what the Lord was saying and believe the Lord God, and they prospered. When they doubted, that's when they got into trouble.

Doubt starts a person on a cycle of fear and confusion, which ultimately leads to murmuring and complaining. The enemy knows the Lord will not allow anyone operating in any of those spirits to prosper, so your adversary will spend a lot of time provoking and inciting you to doubt and to complain against the Lord. James 1:2-8 declares, *"My brethren, count it all joy when ye fall into divers temptations; Knowing this, that the trying of your faith worketh patience. But let patience have her perfect work, that ye may be perfect and entire, wanting nothing. If any of you lack wisdom, let him ask of God, that giveth to all men liberally, and upbraideth not; and it shall be given him. But let him ask in faith, nothing wavering. For he that wavereth is like a wave of the sea driven with the wind and tossed. For let not that man think that he shall receive any thing of the*

Lord. A double minded man is unstable in all his ways." I prefer to believe in God rather than live in fear, doubt, and confusion.

Moreover, some of you are hurt because the Lord didn't give you a blessed marriage with children, a Church building, a broader ministry, a recording contract, a ministry van, a house, employment, healing in your body, or even compensation for your services to Him. Maybe the Lord did not grant salvation to a loved one, and you are hurt. Others appear to be prospering in those areas, but you feel the Lord will not bless you in the same way, even though He said He would. The Lord is no respecter of persons (Romans 2:11). And listen, just because someone you are looking at appears blessed does not mean they did not experience suffering to obtain the blessing.

Moreover, being blessed does not mean they are not going through tests and trials to maintain or hold on to the blessings of the Lord. People say, *"The blessing of the LORD, it maketh rich, and he addeth no sorrow with it"* (Proverbs 10:22). You better dissect that Scripture with the Strong's Concordance to see the true meaning. Sometimes the Lord does add sorrow with a blessing. Just have a baby and then tell me otherwise.

Let me ask: Is it the Lord's will for you to have a building? If not, then why do you feel you need a building? If so, did you save money to purchase or lease a building? Did you take care of your credit so you could qualify for a building or a van? Did you rally the people so they could support the vision for a building or a van? Did you believe the Lord for a building, or did you only focus on worldly requirements? When the Lord says He is going to do something, you do not have to qualify. That thing is done! Furthermore, did you take care of God's house when you had the opportunity? Luke 16:12 clearly informs us, *"And if ye have not been faithful in that which is another man's, who shall give you that which is your own?"*

If you are a psalmist, did you learn your craft? Did you follow the Lord's voice when He placed people in your path to assist you? Did you spend adequate time seeking and worshipping the Lord so He could anoint you to minister? Also, if you desired your family to come to know Jesus, did you earnestly fast and pray for your loved ones to receive salvation? Did you live an upright life in front of your loved ones whom you desired to receive salvation? These are just some examples of saints not doing their part and just waiting for the Lord to bring the promise to pass. I know the Lord is in control, and He has to give humans a heart to do the things they do. However, we can entreat Him to move on our behalf. So we have a role to play in His grand design.

Over the years, I have labored with many of the Lord's children who are so gifted it is unbelievable, and most of them are not doing anything with their gifts or talents. Several received Words concerning the Lord's plan to prosper the works of their hands, yet His plan did not come to pass in their lives. In essence, He has told them to take their gift to the world, and He will prosper their endeavors, but the saints are fearful, lazy, and passive. Many believers sit idle and call it waiting on the Lord and will never see the promises of God come to pass. They say, "If it's God, He'll make it come to pass. God doesn't need my help." No! The Lord has given you the land. He has already opened the door for you to prosper. Just walk through the door. Trust me. You are not waiting on the Lord. He is waiting for you to build on the land He has already given you.

Joshua 18:1-3 declares, *"AND the whole congregation of the children of Israel assembled together at Shiloh, and set up the tabernacle of the congregation there. And the land was subdued before them. And there remained among the children of Israel seven tribes, which had not yet received their inheritance. And Joshua said unto the children of Israel, How long are ye slack to go to possess the land, which the LORD God of your fathers hath given you?"* Seven out of twelve tribes are the majority. You see, if we have not done everything the Lord told us to do to possess our inheritance, we can only blame ourselves when the promises of the Lord are forfeited. I found by experience that no other human has as much power over me as me. The Lord will open doors for you so you can accomplish all He determined for you to complete. Just make sure the thing you are trying to achieve is His will. You also have the power to stop God's will and His move in your life. It's the little things you do or don't do that end up being massive in the grand scheme of your walk with the Lord. Little things like hit or miss obedience or even a lack of integrity.

In the Book of Joshua 7:8-11, the servant of the Lord cried, *"O Lord, what shall I say, when Israel turneth their backs before their enemies! For the Canaanites and all the inhabitants of the land shall hear of it, and shall environ us round, and cut off our name from the earth: and what wilt thou do unto thy great name? And the LORD said unto Joshua, Get thee up; wherefore liest thou thus upon thy face? Israel hath sinned, and they have also transgressed my covenant which I commanded them: for they have even taken of the accursed thing, and have also stolen, and dissembled also, and they have put it even among their own stuff."* The Lord gives precise instructions to us all during our walk with Him. He doesn't always say why He tells us to do something specific, yet it usually lines up with Scripture. Failing to follow His instructions will have far-reaching consequences. Dissembled (3584 Hb.) means: to be untrue in word or deed; to deal falsely.

The Lord gave Israel specific instructions concerning the spoils of war, and one man decided to do something else, and the whole nation suffered. Some even lost their lives during the battle with Ai. You know there is something the Lord told you to do, but you did not do it. He told you again, and you did not do it. Jesus told you again, and again, and again, and you still did your own thing. What the Lord didn't tell you is there would be specific consequences for your disobedience. I'm going somewhere with this.

Many are hurt in the Churches today because they feel they have poured so much into the house of God until they have nothing left for themselves. Yet the Word of God declares in Acts 20:35, *"I have shewed you all things, how that so labouring ye ought to support the weak, and to remember the words of the Lord Jesus, how he said, It is more blessed to give than to receive."* I know if you are a blessing to the Lord's house, the Lord will bless you. That is if you give with the right heart, mind, and spirit. When the Lord declares He loves a cheerful giver, He means it (2nd Corinthians 9:7). I have given much and taken in much. When I did not walk right before the Lord, I took in little, and frankly, the Lord stirred up a lot of mess in my life to get my attention. You must not only give; you must walk in all the Lord's commands, like the command to forgive. I have seen hardships come upon ministries and leaders because there was some sin in their lives, and they did not put the pieces together. No one discerned the trouble they were experiencing was because the Lord was displeased with them, whether for blatant sin, disobedience, or oppressing His children.

When we do not do what the Lord instructs us to do, it is a sin. When we know to do good and doeth it not, it is a sin (James 4:17). When we do not walk in faith, it is a sin (Romans 14:23 c-only). Additionally, the Bible declares, *"In the day of prosperity be joyful, but in the day of adversity consider: God also hath set the one over against the other, to the end that man should find nothing after him"* (Ecclesiastes 7:14). What's more, Job 2:10 c-d declares, *"What? shall we receive good at the hand of God, and shall we not receive evil?"* Since the Scriptures declare all that and you agree, why are you hurt because your expectations have gone unfulfilled?

"When the people therefore saw that Jesus was not there, neither his disciples, they also took shipping, and came to

241

Capernaum, seeking for Jesus. And when they had found him on the other side of the sea, they said unto him, Rabbi, when camest thou hither? Jesus answered them and said, Verily, verily, I say unto you, Ye seek me, not because ye saw the miracles, but because ye did eat of the loaves, and were filled. Labour not for the meat which perisheth, but for that meat which endureth unto everlasting life, which the Son of man shall give unto you: for him hath God the Father sealed" (John 6:24-27). I know you are not serving the Lord just for the fish and the loaves, are you? Are you? If not, then get up and do something with what the Lord placed in your hands. Let go of the anger and put your hands to the plow and do His will in the Earth, and make it count. Make sure you bring His Kingdom glory.

And, if you have fallen in your walk with the Lord and you feel there is no recovery, Repent! Perhaps the Lord will have mercy on you. You will not know the goodness of His mercy unless you Repent and do something different than what you were doing before you got into trouble with the Lord. Even if you can make some things right, you still can't change what has already happened, so move forward. The Lord never turns away from anyone who sincerely Repents! Micah 7:18-19 is true, *"Who is a God like unto thee, that pardoneth iniquity, and passeth by the transgression of the remnant of*

242

his heritage? he retaineth not his anger for ever, because he delighteth in mercy. He will turn again, he will have compassion upon us; he will subdue our iniquities; and thou wilt cast all their sins into the depths of the sea."

Many saints let the enemy steal their joy and peace. The Word declares, *"for the joy of the LORD is your strength"* (Nehemiah 8:10 h-only). If you lose your joy, everything else will soon follow, including your integrity, blessings, hopes, and all the Lord's plans for your life, because the gladness of the Lord is your fortified place, defense, and stronghold. His joy keeps you sane daily. If you go insane, you will lose everything, and if you are married and you and your spouse go crazy together, you are really in trouble. What I'm saying is we can only blame ourselves for the promises of God not being fulfilled. You will never have a valid case if you are blaming the Lord. He cannot be brought up on charges. His seat as a magistrate is above every court. The only thing you can do is look in the mirror.

Although unintentional, saints allow Church hurt to hinder them from walking in the Word of God. Many saints look around years after experiencing Church hurt, and they find they are stuck in a rut, feeling as if there was nothing they could do to cause or persuade

243

the Lord to bless them. Yes, the Lord has given you many things, but His more excellent plan never comes to fruition. Talk about the long-term effects of Church hurt. The Lord told me to write this book so that He can spare you from the pain associated with unforgivingness. Let the pain and injury go before it ruins you. I know some of you are so distressed by not receiving the blessings of the Lord within a specific time frame. So much so that you no longer desire to do the will of God. Now, you believe and feel all your labor in the Lord is in vain. You've waited so long for the blessings of the Lord that you are starting to lose faith and hope. You have to continue to believe He is going to do it for you.

Abraham and Sarah waited so long for a child that Sarah encouraged her husband to bear her a child through her handmaiden (Genesis 16:1-6). Jacob and Rachel did not have children in their early years, so she also looked to her handmaiden to bear children (Genesis 30:1-5). I have seen and heard saints doing some quirky things to bring forth the promises of God in their lives. And when someone does not agree with what the Lord says about that promise, it gets messy.

The Lord told Abraham He would give him a son from his loins and Sarah's womb, yet it was some time later when the promise

244

came to pass. Abraham did not consider it was the Lord's plan for him to receive the promise at 100 years of age (Genesis 15:1-6; 17:15-19; and 21:5). They were only thinking about the natural course of childbearing. They anguished for years about not conceiving, so Sarah had a child through her handmaiden, but it backfired. Before the child was born, she regretted coming up with that plan. I cannot imagine all the years of misery they experienced instead of enjoying their marriage.

One morning, the Lord spoke to me through a song. As I pondered the words to the song, He told me to add the meaning to the song to the book because many of you are repeatedly asking the Lord for something. Maybe you are uttering to the Lord: "If You could just give me this one thing, I will be happy, and I will not ask for anything else. Certainly, my joy will be full." I'm talking about the thing your mind and heart focus on more than anything else. You must have it for your life to be complete. However, the Lord is saying, focus on me; delight your heart in me. Psalm 37:4-5 declares, *"Delight thyself also in the LORD; and he shall give thee the desires of thine heart. Commit thy way unto the LORD; trust also in him; and he shall bring it to pass."* Many people quote parts of that Scripture, but not the most crucial parts: *Delight thyself also in the LORD; commit thy way unto the Lord;* and *trust also in him.*

Please understand you may not have received the thing you long for because it is not time. *"For the vision is yet for an appointed time, but at the end it shall speak, and not lie: though it tarry, wait for it; because it will surely come, it will not tarry"* (Habakkuk 2:3). When you long for something for a lengthy period, it becomes an object of extreme affection. It becomes your idol because you devote time in prayer to make it come to pass. Idolatry is a door for the enemy to cause you unnecessary distress. If the Lord were to grant it to you while you are in the wrong mindset, you would lose yourself completely, including your salvation.

I know of many testimonies where the Lord granted people things they yearned for after a long time, and it went to their heads to the degree they threw it back in the faces of the people who persecuted them for believing the Lord. It displeased the Lord, and He took the blessing away from them. If you desire to receive the blessing to show everyone you are right, you need to let go of it and cleave to the Lord. I mean, truly let it go. Don't consider it at all and focus on the Lord. Stop praying for it, stop longing for it, and stop feeling sad because you didn't get it. Be ready and willing to let it go entirely to build upon your relationship with the Lord. Then you will find a peace you have never experienced before.

Psalms 16:11 declares, *"Thou wilt shew me the path of life: in thy presence is fulness of joy; at thy right hand there are pleasures for evermore."* Do you know when someone loses their god, they go crazy? Laban in Genesis 31:30 lamented concerning his stolen gods: *"And now, though thou wouldest needs be gone, because thou sore longedst after thy father's house, yet wherefore hast thou stolen my gods?"* Idolatry is a serious thing because it takes the place of the Lord in your life and is extremely difficult to release. Idolatry will consume your every thought. You will believe this blessing is the one thing to validate you as a person. You cannot accept living without it. The word idolatry is an immoderate attachment or devotion to something. Your thinking about this particular blessing has caused you to overstep normal boundaries. So now you must find your way back to Jesus.

I would like for you to think about that for a moment. You have lost sight of Jesus, and you need to find your way back. The only way to find your way back to Jesus is to spend time meditating on the Word of God. Are you spending time with the Lord, or are you always asking Him to do something for you? Imagine someone close to you spending time with you regularly, and every time you are together, the person makes the same pleas to you for something specific over and over again. At breakfast, lunch, and dinner, they ask for it. You spend a night out on the town, and they ask for it. While in the car, they ask for it. While taking a walk, they ask for it. While you are away from home on business, they call you and ask for it. It gets so bad that each waking moment entails repeatedly getting in touch with you to ask for the same thing. You reluctantly start a conversation with them because you know they will bring up the subject again.

After a while, you wonder if they like spending time with you or if they are just hanging around so they can get what they lack from you. Now, you are considering what will happen if you grant their request. Well, imagine how the Lord feels when we spend every waking moment thinking about and talking to Him concerning one blessing. We treat Him as if He has no feelings, and His only job is to give us things to make us happy. No, we are to build a relationship with Him. The Lord desires for us to abide in Him. We must place Him first in our lives (Exodus 20:3). He died to complete us and be everything we need (Colossians 2:10).

I understand idolatry. For some of us, the thing we are asking for is just no good for us. It will only cause us deep pain or anguish, and yet we keep asking for it. The Lord will not give it to us because He knows the damage it will do. So, settle it in your mind; the Lord knows what is best. The Lord said in the Book of Jeremiah 29:11-13, *"For I know the thoughts that I think toward you, saith the LORD, thoughts of peace, and not of evil, to give you an expected end. Then shall ye call upon me, and ye shall go and pray unto me, and I will hearken unto you. And ye shall seek me, and find me, when ye shall search for me with all your heart."*

Reader, pray this prayer with me:

Abba, Father, in the name of Jesus Christ of Nazareth, I confess I have not done all I can do to prepare for Your vision for my life. I ask You to forgive me. I also confess I have worshipped the blessing You intended to bestow upon me. Instead of chasing You, I began to pursue the benefits you granted through Christ. I have forgotten all about You because I spend most of my time trying to bring the promises to pass. I ask You to forgive me for neglecting my relationship with You. Abba, Father, I also ask You to forgive me for not walking upright and correct before You. I ask You to forgive me for blaming the Church where You placed me for my stagnation. I confess I hindered myself because I did not obey Your commands to crucify my flesh and its deeds. Lord, reveal to me the things that have hindered me from moving forward so I may get it right with You, in Jesus' name, Amen.

CHAPTER ELEVEN

ARE YOU A JUDGE?

". . . there is none good but one, that is, God."

Mark 10:18 (c-e only)

CHAPTER 11: *ARE YOU A JUDGE?*

Many saints think they have a legitimate complaint against some spiritual leaders in the Body of Christ. These saints are hurt because they feel a spiritual leader betrayed their trust, injured them or a family member, or hurt them in a personal way. Other believers are angry because a leader did not know the Lord's plan for their life and did not release them to do the will of God. Although the grievance may be real, I desire to address why you feel the need to run from the Lord instead of seeking a resolution to the situation. And why does the Lord get the blame for what humans do? Also, why do you feel the need to retaliate?

I realize many believers do not recognize when the Lord has humans doing something to them. I have learned that sometimes humans act out their fleshly weaknesses, and the Lord allows it for a season. What do I mean by fleshly weaknesses? The Bible defines flesh in the Greek (S.C. 4561) as human nature with its frailties and passions, physically or morally, or specifically, carnally minded. Believers forget one crucial truth: spiritual leaders have weaknesses and struggles similar to others in the Church. They are still a work in progress and are yet crucifying the flesh. For example, many leaders are wary of opportunists in the Church and are slow to receive mature believers whom the Lord has newly assigned to a Church. Some leaders struggle with mind battles. And more than a few fall prey to an attack of the adversary. Spiritual leaders are not exempt from life's hardships. Regardless, just because spiritual leaders have weaknesses in their character, it does not mean they are not anointed. Just because you disagree with a man or woman of God, it does not nullify that they are a man or woman of God. And just because they do not handle things the way you think they should, it does not mean the Lord is not with them.

Unfortunately, Church folk seem to think otherwise and assume they will never be offended and feel hurt by leadership in the Church. Unbeknownst to saints, the Lord uses many spiritual leaders unconsciously to mature the saints' character. I'm one such instrument. I only do what the Lord directs me to do, yet someone is always getting offended. However, the Lord told me, *"So many people get offended when you correct them because they feel the conviction of the Holy Ghost."* However, instead of hearing the Lord and correcting themselves, they hold a personal grudge against me. Recently, the Lord told me, *"The world doesn't receive you, but I receive you."*

254

One Sunday morning, many years ago, when I was a new saint, I decided to skip serving in children's Church. I did not inform anyone because I felt they didn't need me since I was just an administrative person who registered the children as they attended the children's service. There were a lot of people scheduled to serve that day. I didn't know how serving in the Church worked, and I didn't know about faithfulness. Instead, I attended the regular Church service and sang in the choir. After the service, I saw someone talking to an Elder and pointing at me. The Elder walked up to me, confirmed my name, and asked me to step aside to talk. Then, he proceeded to correct me so harshly about not serving I cried openly. I felt so bad. I didn't know. Well, he explained that no one showed to help with the children. At the time, two to three hundred children attended children's Church on a regular Sunday. His last words to me were, "DON'T YOU EVER DO THAT AGAIN!" Yes, he spoke in a loud and stern tone, and he is a gentleman.

After I acknowledged the correction and walked away, the sister who gave him the names of everyone who usually worked in children's Church came up to me and said, "Sister Fern, I'm the one who told on you and everyone who did not show up. That was not right what you all did. There were only a few of us there trying to

255

take care of all those children." Instead of getting offended, I wiped my tears and made up my mind never to do that again. What were the odds that no one would show for children's Church on the same day I decided not to show? Zero to one! I took that situation as a direct message from the Lord Jesus, tailor-made for me. The Lord caused all of that because He desired me to be faithful in my service to Him. I did not take it personally or hold a grudge against the Elder or the sister. I knew it was the Lord, and I responded accordingly: corrected and repentant.

However, many saints would not have responded so graciously. They would not have accepted the correction as coming from the Lord. They would have only focused on the person and how they were corrected. I remember correcting a woman about a lack of obedience to her husband. She was relatively new to the ministry. But, she had been in and out of Churches for years, so she thought she knew a lot. She came with the wrong mindset, like we could not teach her anything because in her mind she was already a Minister.

When the Lord had me correct her about her disobedience, she replied, "I'm not disobedient." She openly argued with the Holy Ghost. Once I opened the Scriptures to her, she finally conceded and agreed she was disobedient in many areas. She wept sore because she could not resist the wisdom of the Holy Ghost. After I corrected her, she had a personal problem with me from that point on. I forgot about it because I was just letting the Lord use me. It was not personal. However, she took it personally and talked about me behind my back to other Church members for years and never let it go. She thought it was me correcting her and not the Lord. Later on, she continued to talk about me even after she told me the Lord showed her over and over that I belonged to Him. She could not accept the correction as coming from the Lord. Then one day in service, my husband and I saw a devil possess her. We saw her eyes change to black, and her walk changed to a slow-motion, manly, gliding stride. That night I asked the Lord what spirit it was that entered her, and He said, *"Hatred."* The next day, I spoke with her on the phone; I told her what my husband and I saw at the last Church service and what the Lord said that evening. She responded: "When you said you saw my eyes and walk change, I felt different." Within a week, she left the ministry spewing all manner of evil.

When the Lord chooses leaders, He does not choose them because they are perfect. He picks them because of His desire to select that person. The Lord calls His leaders to specific types of people, and the leader has just what the people need. If you have always manipulated others to get your way, the Lord Jesus will give you a leader you cannot manipulate. He will provide you with leaders who will challenge you to exchange your carnal nature for a spiritual nature.

Nevertheless, some will always have a problem with the Lord's choice. Yes, the Lord always chooses humans to do the work because they can relate to what you are going through. Being human means they will be flawed, and the Lord is fully aware of every shortcoming. Yet, the Lord will use the leader's weaknesses to draw the mess out of your character so you can grow in love, forgiveness, compassion, and mercy. Their imperfections will expose whether you are selfish or arrogant. If you love little, it will be made known. If you are self-righteous, it will come out of your character. If there is sin in your life, it will manifest. If you are a jealous person, the Lord will allow the person you are jealous of to do or say something to you, out of their flawed nature, to see if you will gossip about the person or pray for them. In praying for them, you will be praying for yourself because you cannot change them. The Lord will use these situations to shed light on everyone's shortcomings.

However, the congregation didn't get the memo; their leader will too be a flawed human needing the blood of Jesus Christ to cleanse them from all unrighteousness. Believe me, everyone, including the leaders, will have their season when the Lord desires to work on them. Just as the Lord uses leaders to mature saints, He uses the saints to develop leaders for greater works of service. And some believers thoroughly put their leaders through trying situations. And the leader must continue to pray for them and show love. Leaders have to have a forgiving spirit because they know humans are imperfect. Yet, saints need to have a willingness to forgive as well and understand that leaders are only doing what the Lord would have them to do. If your leader is angry with you, it is a good practice to seek the Lord to find out if the Lord is actually the one angry with you. If you find Jesus is displeased with you, repent! If the Lord is not displeased with you, keep pleasing the Lord; do not concern yourself with what the leader does or says. Just pass your test.

So, since the Church is full of flawed humans, we must fully follow Scripture to remedy divisive situations and restore the saints to peace. Sometimes, it seems the circumstances will never end, and the Lord is not answering your prayers to tell the leader how you feel or to back off of you. The Lord is not answering your prayers because He is using the situation to mature you and draw you closer to Him. Unfortunately, many do not allow the Lord to complete the work.

259

Instead of allowing the Lord to work on you, there is a strong desire to leave the Church. Sometimes people backslide because they think someone is purposefully doing them harm. But it is not the leader doing anything to you. The Lord is trying to mature you.

When the Lord instructs someone to begin a ministry, depending on the manner of people assigned to them, there will be a severe spiritual battle to deliver the people they are called to from the powers of darkness. New saints require continuous prayer and personal attention. Ministry is work. Eliminating distractions is one reason the Lord directs His servants to separate from family. I did not grow up in the Church. So, for me to accept correction was incredibly humbling. During deliverance, those you minister to may struggle with mind battles or outright lies about you and your ministry. No matter how sincere you are, the enemy, the world, and the person's flesh will fight day and night to keep the person bound. One of the main things they will have difficulty understanding is the principle of the tailor-made test. Ministry is all about character building and deliverance. If they never come to understand that principle, they will run.

The Problem with running is that once you start, you will always run whenever someone at a ministry hurts your feelings, especially since the same tests will keep coming around repeatedly. The test is often to see if we will yield and submit to the Lord's authority in the Earth. I know one thing: adversity is always used and allowed by the Lord to show us something inside ourselves. His leaders are only doing what He is leading them to do concerning us, and we get offended. Sometimes the leader is being led unknowingly by the Lord to address your character's specific area, which is too painful for you to face. So you say the leader is doing this or that. If we get the courage to hold on to the Scriptures, we will save ourselves from heartaches, and then we will grow spiritually. If you do not allow the Church to be an instrument to change your character, the Lord will use the world, and you will get whipped.

Change is often a challenge for many. It is easy to stay as you are, but change is difficult. The flesh does not like to change. It is comfortable fulfilling its lusts and will kick and scratch to keep it that way. All the while, the Holy Ghost inside of you is saying, *"Change! Be Renewed!"* We ask the Lord to help us, and when He does, we reject His help. However, if you think about it carefully, you will realize that the issue with the leader is the same problem you are fighting the Lord on concerning yourself. It is the very thing the Lord is trying to change, correct, and mature in your life so He can use you more.

I hear someone saying, but it hurts so badly! I know. If it didn't hurt, then it is probably not something you need to change. If you are dead to it, why would you be working on it? If you have crucified that area of your character, why would the Lord require you to work on it? The sign you need to work on it is the hurt and pain you feel because of it. Listen, I know the Lord will use anyone and everything necessary to mature your character. He loves you that much. He will leave no stone unturned. His goal is to save you from condemnation. 1st Corinthians 11:31-32 declares, *"For if we would judge ourselves, we should not be judged. But when we are judged, we are chastened of the Lord, that we should not be condemned with the world."* But, if you are not growing in the Lord, then you are stagnated and fruitless. If you are not bearing fruit, you are of no use to the Lord's Kingdom. But, he desires you to bear fruit. John 15:16 declares, *"Ye have not chosen me, but I have chosen you, and ordained you, that ye should go and bring forth fruit, and that your fruit should remain: that whatsoever ye shall ask of the Father in my name, he may give it you."*

Two stories in the Books of Genesis chapters 29-31 and 1st Samuel chapters 18-27 depict Jacob's deceptive relationship with his uncle Laban and David's tumultuous relationship with King Saul, respectively. These Biblical accounts speak to the Lord's nature to choose a person when they are immature, allowing them to grow by life's tests. When the Lord chooses someone for ministry, it does not imply they do not have flaws in their character. The Lord works on our shortcomings, often using those in authority over us as instruments of perfection. The Lord was actively working amid both situations to bring about the character-building He desired in Jacob and David.

We know the Lord was actively working in the two accounts because when David desired to take matters into his own hands and harm Saul, he felt convicted and smote in his heart. David knew he was wrong for the condition of his heart and cried out to Saul to rectify the situation. David considered and declared: How can I lift my hand against the Lord's anointed and be guiltless? Reader, how can a person put their thoughts and mouth on the Lord's anointed and be guiltless? Whether you agree with how your leader handled you or not, the Lord chose them to lead you. If you turn and do them harm, you will find yourself fighting against the Lord.

On the contrary, when the Lord told Jacob to leave his uncle's house, Laban and his men pursued him. Then in the evening, while Laban and the men were resting, the Lord spoke to Laban in a dream instructing him, *". . . Take heed that thou speak not to Jacob either good or bad"* Genesis 31:24. In other words, the Lord told Laban, Jacob's uncle, father-in-law, and employer, *"Do not touch my servant."* In the two examples I mentioned, the Lord could have stepped in and caused specific events to cease, but instead, He allowed David to be on the run from King Saul for nearly two decades. He also allowed Laban to mistreat Jacob for over twenty years. However, in both instances, the principal parties, David (2nd Samuel 1:11-12) and Jacob (Genesis 33:10-11), came to understand humility and were learning to build upon their relationship with the Lord. They were learning to trust the Lord. You do not have to take matters into your own hands. The Lord will settle the issue at the appointed time, whether peaceably or otherwise.

One of the most therapeutic things you can do instead of leaving a Church is to meet with your spiritual leaders to settle misunderstandings. You will learn a lot if you sit down with your leaders instead of finding fault with them. True leaders chosen by the Lord will receive you and give you an answer to what ails you, but they will not bite their tongue. It will be time to face the truth. The Lord will also give you an understanding of what He is doing in your life. It may be difficult to hear some of the things the Lord will use them to share with you, yet if you listen, you will come to understand it is the Lord attempting to reshape and remold you through the tests and trials you are facing. If the leader has to yell or be uncouth with you, it means you are refusing to change.

When something is going on in our lives, we do not always realize we are the problem. Most of the time, Jesus is encouraging us so we will not give up, yet encouragement does not suggest we are pleasing in the Lord's sight. Sometimes, we fail to see we are wrong when we are repetitively encouraged. All that encouragement keeps us from correcting ourselves. That is not to say the leaders are not in the wrong. However, it is unlikely they are in every case. For instance, I remember someone in the Church saying a leader was wrong in how they handled a situation. They openly yelled at the leader, accusing them of wrongdoing. They were looking to find fault with the leader and finally found something they could use. They could not see their role in the matter, although there were witnesses. As the leader listened attentively to the person's complaint, surprisingly, the leader stepped up and said, "If you feel I have done you wrong, forgive me." Everyone became silent. What an example!

The person was so shocked it was like their mouth was hanging open. They did not expect that response. They desired an argument. They intended to humiliate the leader. But God! The leader's forgiving spirit came forth and squashed the matter. All eyes were now on the accuser. Everyone was waiting for an answer. All the person could say is, "I forgive you." They had to let it go. Disagreement resolved. We have to bear responsibility for our actions and not be in the habit of blaming others when we are going through something. The Lord was trying to do something in the person's life, but they resisted the Holy Ghost.

Besides, the Scriptures declare, *"For we wrestle not against flesh and blood, but against principalities, against powers, against the rulers of the darkness of this world, against spiritual wickedness in high places"* Ephesians 6:12. Did you notice the word against has the term again at its core? The Scriptures warn us that unseen forces will attack again and again and again and again, and they will increase in authority as they strike. These forces will also attack more aggressively. If it is not one thing, there will be another, so running from conflict is not the answer.

266

Also, keep in mind, those in leadership positions are often misunderstood and experience the brunt of vicious gossip. I keep mentioning gossipmongers in the Church because it is a terrible, menacing soul-eating disease. When things go wrong in the Church, the leader bears the weight, not the laity. The Minister is the first one to pick up the slack when finances are lacking. Shepherds accept the blame when soul winning is challenging. Also, the preacher suffers shame and reproach if believers are not living right in the sight of the world. Preachers often wear the label hypocrite because of the lifestyles of their members. Not only do Ministers suffer from gossip, they often suffer from low approval from the very souls they labor to disciple as if they are politicians.

No matter what type of leader Church folk have, there will always be someone who has an issue with their leadership, as they did with Moses and Aaron. The congregation always complained regarding their leadership, and Moses was the meekest man upon the face of the Earth (Numbers 12:3). If you are one of those who are gossiping about your leaders instead of praying for them, then you will be like a stench in the leader's nostrils, and the Lord will cause it to be so because you are a stench in the Lord's nostrils. If the leaders are hard on you, then there is something in you that you are refusing to change, and the Lord knows. As long as flaws remain in your character, it will be difficult for you to fellowship with the Lord.

There have been times when the Lord used me to be gentle with some and hard on others. What I have learned is if I'm hard on someone, they need it. If I'm gentle with someone, they need it. The Lord uses me how He desires. I'm even hard on myself, though the Lord is kind to me. He doesn't deal with me on the level I deserve. Yet, when He does deal with me, I'm humbled. Sometimes I desire to have a pity party and blame others who are in authority over me. But, when I stop to consider, I realize it is me and not them. Then I confess it is the Lord trying to work something in me and not the leaders picking on me.

Joseph came to understand when he was in Egypt that it was the Lord who drove his brothers to sell him into slavery so His plan could go forth in Joseph's life. Genesis 45:4-5 declares, *"And Joseph said unto his brethren, Come near to me, I pray you. And they came near. And he said, I am Joseph your brother, whom ye sold into Egypt. Now therefore be not grieved, nor angry with yourselves, that ye sold me hither: for God did send me before you to preserve life."*

In times of reflection, I realize it is inevitable for spiritual leaders to have Church hurt, and they may struggle to stay encouraged. The only thing is their struggles are private, and you may never get to know about them, especially if the Lord cannot trust you to pray for their strength. I'm not talking about sin, yes sin may be a problem too, but I'm talking about the effects of disharmony or disunity in the Church. It causes the vision to suffer, making their labor seem worthless. I'm talking about the family struggles leaders experience because many leaders neglect their spouses and children for the Church. Yes, leaders have struggles too. Much prayer and compassion will go a long way for spiritual leaders and their families.

Whatever the situation, everyone needs to pray and fast so all may heal as a Church. The saddest thing I have seen in a ministry is when many people are hurting because of unresolved conflict, and no one is praying or walking in the Word of God. Instead, everyone is complaining, murmuring, gossiping, accusing, lying, stirring up strife, and creating division. For that reason, Matthew 18:15-17 commands, *"Moreover if thy brother shall trespass against thee, go and tell him his fault between thee and him alone: if he shall hear thee, thou hast gained thy brother. But if he will not hear thee, then take with thee one or two more, that in the mouth of two or three witnesses every word may be established. And if he shall neglect to hear them, tell it*

269

unto the church: but if he neglect to hear the church, let him be unto thee as an heathen man and a publican."

The Lord never promised there would not be conflict. However, it is the Lord's will for the saints to get issues resolved. It is vital to the Church that we forgive. So for your own sake, don't let another day go by with you holding on to old Church hurt. Let it go! And if you can make it right, make it right! Reconciliation is critical because the Lord said He would not receive your offering until you resolve disputes. *"But I say unto you, That whosoever is angry with his brother without a cause shall be in danger of the judgment: . . . Therefore if thou bring thy gift to the altar, and there rememberest that thy brother hath ought against thee; Leave there thy gift before the altar, and go thy way; first be reconciled to thy brother, and then come and offer thy gift"* (Matthew 5:22-24).

My final words are for those who are calling leaders in the Church hypocrites. You need to follow the instructions given in 2nd Chronicles 7:14, *"If my people, which are called by my name, shall humble themselves, and pray, and seek my face, and turn from their wicked ways; then will I hear from heaven, and will forgive their sin, and will heal their land."* If you are critical of spiritual leaders, then I chalk that up to you being immature concerning leadership. I know you are immature because I was like that once. The Lord told me to tell you: *"Many of you do not have the character to sit in the presence of Godly men and women of great authority because you refuse to walk in a way that is pleasing to the Lord. You refuse to walk in Scripture. It is the same today as it was with Moses and the children of Israel; only two men out of millions pleased the Lord. Since you refuse to walk in the Lord's ways and honor His authority in the Earth, He will drive you out of their presence. When you backslide and leave a ministry, the Lord is driving you out of His servant's sight. You are not the one leaving. The Lord is pushing you out of His House because of all your murmuring, complaining, and gossiping. Instead of looking at yourself, you keep talking, adding sin to sin* (Isaiah 30:1). *If you do not repent, you will perish with the world, saith the Lord."*

It is challenging to be a spiritual leader. There is no other position of authority that requires a continuous intense battle with evil spiritual forces. Being a spiritual leader is a matter of life and death, especially since preachers are intercessors and prayer warriors. They endure a lot of attacks meant for those in the congregation. A spiritual leader is in an eternal position; meaning, they sit in the spirit realm. They are spiritual. Everything they do and say is spiritual and has

271

deeper ramifications, whether good or bad. Therefore, they need a lot of prayer. So, stop complaining, correct yourself, and pray for your Church leaders to have the strength to complete the Lord's will.

Note, you are not praying to change your leaders. The Lord already made them who they are, and your prayers are not to manipulate them or the Lord, nor is it to correct them because the Lord already shaped and molded them to be how He desires for them to be. Their sole responsibility is to please the Lord, not you. Likewise, He made you a certain way, and your sole responsibility is to please the Lord and not man. Prayer will strengthen you to take correction and build your inner man. When you pray instead of complaining and gossiping, you are praying for yourself to receive wisdom to humble yourself to accept the leaders the Lord gave you, which will be to your benefit. When you receive your leaders, you receive the Lord. Hebrews 13:17-18 declares, *"Obey them that have the rule over you, and submit yourselves: for they watch for your souls, as they that must give account, that they may do it with joy, and not with grief: for that is unprofitable for you. Pray for us: for we trust we have a good conscience, in all things willing to live honestly.*

Reader, pray this prayer with me:

Abba, Father, in the name of Jesus Christ of Nazareth, I know I'm in deep trouble with You for my mindset concerning Your menservants and maidservants. I have not given honor where honor was due, and I railed on and gossiped about the leaders You gave me instead of receiving them. I acknowledge I murmured and complained, instead of understanding Your servants were placed in my life to develop my character. Now, I know, You assigned specific leaders to fulfill a duty concerning me, and nothing that transpired was personal. Lord, I beg You, please forgive me! I know I've been suffering the consequences of my actions, but I'm pleading for Your mercy right now. I know I don't deserve it, but Your Word declares You delight in granting mercy in Jesus' name. Amen!

CHAPTER TWELVE

THE BROKEN FAMILY TREE

"For I am come to set a man at variance against his father, and the daughter against her mother, and the daughter in law against her mother in law."

Matthew 10:35

CHAPTER 12: *THE BROKEN FAMILY TREE*

Another form of Church hurt for the believer is when the Lord orchestrates a separation between families, saved and unsaved, to set aside some to a greater purpose. The broken family tree represents broken natural and Church families. *"He that loveth father or mother more than me is not worthy of me: and he that loveth son or daughter more than me is not worthy of me. And he that taketh not his cross, and followeth after me, is not worthy of me"* (Matthew 10:37-38).

Based on Scripture, if you do not separate from those the Lord requires you to separate from, you will never reach your calling, and you will not receive the Kingdom of Heaven. I do not know of anyone who was attached to their family members more than me. I love my natural family very much. I also loved my first spiritual family. Unfortunately, my attachment to my family was just as it was with the ministry. I did not desire to leave. But, the Lord Jesus was calling me to a higher calling and a more excellent work. It was not His will for me to remain a layperson for the rest of my life.

Based on my personal and ministerial experience, I have found Matthew 10:37-38 to be one of the most challenging Scriptures for believers to swallow. Many do not believe it is the Lord Jesus requiring them to leave their natural and spiritual family to follow and serve Him. They refuse to accept the Scriptures. They do not understand the Lord when He says they will not be worthy of the Kingdom of Heaven. They think they can serve the Lord on their terms. Well, I'm telling you, God's Word is true. If you do not do your Father's will, which is in Heaven, you will not receive the Kingdom of Heaven. There is no if, and, or but about it. *"Not every one that saith unto me, Lord, Lord, shall enter into the kingdom of heaven; but he that doeth the will of my Father which is in heaven. Many will say to me in that day, Lord, Lord, have we not prophesied in thy name? and in thy name have cast out devils? and in thy name done many wonderful works? And then will I profess unto them, I never knew you: depart from me, ye that work iniquity"* (Matthew 7:21-23).

When the Lord was calling me out of the ministry where I gave my life to Jesus nearly seven years earlier, I started having night dreams that I left the ministry to do something remarkable. They were not dreams of backsliding. In the dreams, I was at another Church where I did not recognize anyone. Now, I know I was married to the leader. Yet, at the time, the Lord did not allow me to discern that piece of information. I also had several dreams of storms and tornadoes with crowds of people in the way of its path. My future husband and I were ministering to hundreds of people, leading them to safety in a house. In the dreams, we had a ministry in our home, filled with people from the basement to the living room. All who believed our warning found safety away from the path of the tornado. I'm talking about tornadoes that appeared to be a mile wide and tremendously dark. When I awoke, I pondered the meaning of my dreams. I knew I was not going to be at that ministry much longer.

As a side note, in the early days, and still today, the saints had Church in their homes (Acts 2:1-4, Acts 5:42, Acts 28:30-31, 1st Corinthians 16:19, Colossians 4:15, and Philemon 1:2). More importantly, Jesus' platform was often in someone's home. In truth, He frequently ministered to multitudes while in someone's house (Matthew 8:14-16, Mark 2:1-12, Luke 19:5-10).

One thing I noticed, when I had a mind to leave too soon, the Lord sent a sister in the Church to tell me she dreamed I was in another Church. She told me, in her dream, I said to myself: "The Holy Ghost is not here! I have to get out of here! I looked around, and then, she said, I gathered my things and got up and left." Her dream helped me to wait on Jesus to fulfill His plan in my life. It was not for me to leave to join another Church because the Lord was calling me to ministry with my husband. Then someone prophesied to me that they saw me leaving the Church. I knew it was the Lord because I had seen it in dreams. However, they began to interpret what they heard and accused the devil of using someone to get me out of the Church. I knew the Lord was showing them I would leave, yet He didn't show them it was His plan and not the devil's plan.

See, I was a person whom the Lord talked to throughout my life, even though I did not know Him by name. I would see things that were going to happen in the future. For instance, when I was a freshman in college, I saw a vision of myself running from a young man while walking to my dorm room. I couldn't see the person's face; nevertheless, I ran as fast as possible to my dorm room door while trying to get out my keys to open the door. If I recall, I dropped my keys, and the person launched at me, grabbing my arm. The vision ended. After seeing that, I immediately thought someone is going to attack me, and I needed to practice running to my dorm room and entering without any mishaps like dropping the keys.

I practiced for two weeks, and then what I saw happened; only this time, I made it to my room door and did not drop my keys; I entered my room safely but it was just in the nick of time. When the Lord gave me instructions, I followed Him, even though I did not know it was Him. When I called upon Him, I know that He helped me, and I wasn't professing Jesus Christ as Lord and Saviour, nor was I raised in the Church. Some people call it intuition; gut feeling; inside voice; somehow, I knew; something said; or something told me. No, it was the Lord; His hand was upon me, and that could not be changed by anyone, including the adversary. It was ordained for me to serve Jesus Christ. The Lord recently confirmed to my husband that He was speaking to me when I was young. However, I still needed to give my life to Jesus and confess Him as Lord and Saviour. Romans 11:29 declares, *"For the gifts and calling of God are without repentance."*

One form of blasphemy is when the Lord says He is going to do something in someone's life, and another person who claims to be a believer comes along and attributes that thing that the Lord is going to do or has done to the adversary. Many saints miss it when they try to interpret dreams or what the Lord is saying without asking the Lord. Don't ever attempt to figure out what the Lord is doing because it is very easy to blaspheme. He is not a God we can decipher!

I also had all manner of dreams about my natural family, which indicated the Lord's plan to sever my relationship. Yet, I didn't understand. The person who prophesied that they saw me leaving the

Church also gave me a word of knowledge about my family. The word was so accurate that it was the same conversation the Lord had with me weeks earlier. However, I was still attached. When my future husband came, he mentioned the possibility of moving to another country when we married. I cried because I could not imagine leaving my family.

Nonetheless, one day the Lord had someone at the Church walk up to me and whisper: *"You are a manpleaser!"* I replied, what did you say? They stepped to me and said, *"You heard me. The Lord told me to tell you that you are a manpleaser!"* I was appalled, but it was true. For two months, during that time, the Lord had told me to leave the youth department permanently. I worked faithfully in that area for nearly four years and was excited about the Lord sending me to join the evangelism team and Christian education department. However, I had to wait for approval from leadership to serve on those auxiliaries. I was excited about the spiritual promotion, yet I was afraid to tell the person over the youth ministry the Lord had released me from that auxiliary. I was fearful of what he was going to say. Yes! I was a manpleaser. Now that I think about it, I did not even consider what Jesus would say or do if I did not please Him. I did eventually muster the courage to resign from the youth ministry and move forward.

Then one day, about five months later, I was walking through my bedroom praying, and the Lord said, *"Prepare yourself for ministry."* I said, Lord, they are not going to let me minister. Then He said, *"I'm about to bring whirlwind change into your life."* I immediately thought: Hallelujah! I was excited. Then I considered, Whirlwind? A whirlwind tears up everything in its path. What's going to happen? The Lord was setting the stage for change to come forth in my life, and there was nothing I could do to stop it. Then, the Lord said, *"I'm going to send you and so and so a husband this year."* I told so and so what the Lord said about her husband coming by the end of the year, and, by golly, she was married by year's end.

Ten months after the Lord spoke that to me, He sent my future husband from Europe. Shortly after his arrival, the Lord instructed him to attend services at the Church where I attended. After being in the Church for five days, the Lord instructed him to participate in an evangelism meeting on Friday. I was an evangelism team leader and one of the secretaries, so I usually arrived early to sit in the front so I could hear and take notes. On that particular day, I was running late and sat next to a brother who was new at the ministry. Then the Lord spoke to me and said, *"This man shall be your husband."*

Now, I can see the importance of leaving the youth department to join the evangelism team. When I worked with the youth, I barely attended regular services because I was always in the basement with the children. My future husband probably would have never seen me. Five months later, I had a dream we were dating, and everyone in the Church was against him, even though the Church leader permitted us to date. In the dream, I stood up and began to defend him, but it didn't matter. The saints in my dream disliked the man the Lord sent to be my husband. They didn't believe he was to marry me, but the Lord did place him in my life and chose me to be his wife.

It is like that with many families in the Church. The Lord has a plan for someone to leave a ministry to start their ministerial journey, and the family members, spiritual and natural, fight against the move. That is why the Lord told my future spouse not to share with anyone at the Church that he was Apostolic Prophetic authority. Notwithstanding, he was surprised when nine people on different occasions told him the Lord shared with them who he was.

When the Lord says to leave a Church, it will always be for an important assignment. The Lord always does greater. He is the God of increase. And the Lord is not speaking about the number of people. Sometimes the work is more complicated or challenging. Jesus said, *"Verily, verily, I say unto you, He that believeth on me, the works that I do shall he do also; and greater works than these shall he do; because I go unto my Father"* (John 14:12). As time goes on, evil will increase, so those whom the Lord chooses must prepare to do something significant so that grace can abound, for the battle will be progressively fierce.

Again, when the person whom the Lord is calling has the strength to resist those who oppose the change, many who disagree become angry, confused, bitter, violent, and unforgiving. They will adamantly say it's not the Lord. When they say it's not the Lord, that very thing they say is not the Lord is Him. Anyone who says it is not Him doesn't know Him because they would not put anything past Him, especially when they know His Word. Only religious people repeatedly recite the phrase, "That's not God." The Lord has not called us to be religious or self-righteous. A person who has a relationship with Him will just keep their mouths shut lest they bring trouble upon themselves. And understand this, the very person you think is not worthy of being called is the person the Lord is calling (1st Corinthians 1:26).

In the Book of Genesis 37:5-11, Joseph was met with opposition when he told his family about his dreams and the Lord's plan for his life. Israel asked: Are you saying you will be greater than us all? Then he considered and held his peace. The Lord had not told Joseph's parents or his siblings what He had planned for Joseph. In truth, Joseph was the one who always revealed the Lord's plan, and Joseph was ultimately the one who explained what it all meant when his brothers came to Egypt to buy food (Genesis 42-45). My point is if you are expecting the Lord to tell you what He has planned for someone else's life, you may be waiting a long time. You have to talk to the person the Lord has chosen to find out what is going on, and even then, you will not find out precisely what the Lord has planned. There is no other way to know what the Lord intends except to live out His plan.

Listen, I know what I am talking about because I have not only experienced the same thing happen to me, but I have unknowingly done the same thing to others. When I was young and ignorant of the Lord, I spent years praying for certain things **to** happen, and they did not happen. I also prayed for certain things **not** to happen, and they happened anyway. The Lord allowed these prayers so He could teach me a valuable lesson about prayer and His will. As much as we like to believe we are in control, we are not. The Lord is the only one in control, and His will is the only thing that will come to pass in the Earth and your life.

In any event and contrary to popular belief, Church leaders do not require disciples to separate from family members. When the Lord requires it and impresses upon the believer to separate, many ask, "If we separate from them, how can they be saved?" The Lord desires all men to be saved (1st Timothy 2:4), including all of our family members, but you are assuming the Lord's plan is for them to receive salvation through you, which is not always the case. Since we all belong to the Lord, He can at anytime call us out of a Church or a family to fulfill His greater purpose, which we have no idea of, and there is no age limit on when He will call us out. There is no limit on who He will call. He calls both genders and all nations of people.

Parents cannot say to an almighty God: My child is too young to be a Minister. The children belong to the Lord, so He will do as He will with them. Even as He did with the Prophet Samuel in 1st Samuel 2:18, which declares, *"But Samuel ministered before the LORD, being a child, girded with a linen ephod."* A Church leader cannot say to an almighty God the person has no experience or does not fit the script of what they believe is a leader. The leader cannot say to the Lord, "But I'm in authority over them. They have to listen to me. I still have to train them." They cannot tell a mighty God, "Lord, you have to run that by me first. I have to release them." I have heard all of these things. But, the truth is there are no prerequisites or stipulations. The Lord calls, and we answer. It's that simple.

When individuals agree to follow the Lord, the family members and Church members, in their anger, often blaspheme against the Holy Ghost by saying, "That's the devil telling you to start a ministry" **(TRUE STORY)**. The Scripture declares, *"In the multitude of words there wanteth not sin: but he that refraineth his lips is wise"* (Proverbs 10:19). That type of opposition creates a fiery environment for individuals who are merely obeying and following the Lord. All who give their lives to Jesus under their leadership also experience unnecessary persecution from family members and the Church. Persecution is expected from unbelievers, but the Church? Usually, true believers will pray for the work to go forth instead of praying for it to fail. It is better not to pray at all if you do not understand what the Lord is doing. Praying for the work of the Lord to fail is witchcraft. Someone is going to give an account to an almighty God for all those troubled souls. Acts 5:39 warns, *"But if it be of God, ye cannot overthrow it; lest haply ye be found even to fight against God."* Those called out of these families and Churches have to guard their hearts carefully to make sure they do not become angry and bitter amid the new work. Forgive quickly so the Lord can continue to use you. Family members and Church members must also let it go. *"Keep thy heart with all diligence; for out of it are the issues of life"* (Proverbs 4:23). Life in that passage of Scripture means congregation life (S.C. 2416).

Some leaders speak ill of those called to start a ministry. If you hear something and begin talking about those people because your leader was unsure of what the Lord was doing, you will bring hardship upon yourself and your family. It is best to guard your relationship with the Lord and stay out of it. They left, the leader said, "Don't support or have contact with them!" It is over. Let it go and stay in your lane. The Lord will bring all things to light in His time. Staying in your lane is an excellent way to guard your heart against the negative side of congregational life. Praying for the Church you left behind is another way to protect your heart. Pray instead of gossiping. And I also learned the hard way, don't say anything, good or bad, because your words will be twisted and misunderstood by the hearers.

Listen, I know what I'm talking about because it happened to me when the Lord sent my husband. He was already in ministry in Europe, and no one considered I had a ministerial calling. Some thought my calling was only to the ministry of helps because I had administrative skills. That was partly right because I am called to be my husband's helpmeet. Regrettably, the Lord did not let them know of my calling to something greater. Yet, the Lord told me by many dreams and direct verbal communication that I had a calling on my life.

I remember having dreams of being a Psalmist, and a sister in the Church came and told me they also dreamed about me being a Psalmist. I did not share my dreams with them, but I listened. As they explained, I noted the Lord gave us the same dream. Now, the Lord has granted me to write over one hundred songs, some of which I sing in ministry. Also, I did not know of my calling to be a Minstrel. In 2019, the Lord said, *"You will learn the keyboard. I AM teaching you the keyboard so you can add music to your songs."* Only my husband and mother knew I was supposed to be playing the piano. When I was a child, age six, my mother taught me some simple songs on the piano. She was surprised I remembered how to play after showing me one time. I don't know why she was so surprised because it was in my blood. Her mother, who was a devout Christian, played the organ and sang at her Church. At age fourteen, my mother purchased me a small digital organ. I played that organ until it stopped working. Although it was not time, I understood how to play, but since I did not know it was the Lord's will for me to play, I never perfected my craft. And frankly, I forgot all about those occasions until the Lord brought it back to my remembrance while writing this book.

I remember the Lord waking me up one day shortly after I gave my life to Jesus, calling me, *"Evangelist, Evangelist. I AM going to give you a husband."* Then I said, Oh Lord! It can just be You and me. Why do I have to have a husband? He responded, *"Because where I AM taking you, you can't go alone."* No one knew. I remember always praying and interceding, and the Lord showed me the Prophetess calling upon my life. I did not understand a person could hold two offices. What the Lord was showing me at the time didn't make any sense. Why was the Lord saying on one occasion, *"Evangelist,"* and another time, He was showing me *"Prophetess?"*

Years later, I posed a general question to a believer who could see people's callings. I asked, "What does a person do when they know they are called to be a Prophetess?" They responded, "Is the person ready to walk in that calling?" I replied, No! They then said, "If they are not ready, they should keep it to themselves." Well, now I know it was not meant for me to tell the leaders. Three years later, without me saying anything about my calling, my future husband explained how he saw my calling as a Prophetess Evangelist, holding two offices. Besides that, when it was time for me to leave the Church, a few others who also had callings on their lives told me they saw I was a Prophetess and Evangelist.

If I had not discerned that the Lord was releasing me from the Church I was faithfully attending, I would not have accomplished all the things I was supposed to accomplish. Think about this: I was content at the time with an associate's degree. It is not important for me to be somebody well-known, but it is important for me to do God's will. I often had dreams I was walking across the stage at various graduation ceremonies. I had no plans to pursue more degrees, so I did not think about it. Some time went by; then, my future husband, who knew nothing of me at the time, gave me a Word of the Lord, *"I see you getting many more degrees. The Lord said you are going to go all the way."* Even though I had the dreams, I did not tell him. Instead, I said, I'm not thinking about school. I'm done with school. He repeated the word and said, *"You will go back to school and get many more degrees."* He did not even know I had an associate's degree.

Four years later, the Lord told me to go back to school. I received my bachelor's degree and then my master's degree. After earning my master's degree, I remembered, years earlier, a different Man of God telling me I would have a master's degree in ten years. He told me that when I only had an associate's degree. I counted the years, and it was exactly ten years from the time he gave me the Word of the Lord that I received my master's. After the master's, I finally earned my PhD. No one knew the Lord planned to advance me to a PhD level education and have me teach at a foreign university.

Additionally, I remember when I received a word from a visiting Prophet from Africa. He said, *"I see you doing something with your hands, and it is going to be so profitable for you."* Immediately following service, a sister in the Church said, "Sister Fern, the Lord said, *"You will be writing books; that's what you will be doing with your hands."* I looked at her strangely, like she missed it. I thought: Me, writing books? I don't know the first thing about writing a book. Then she said, "You know, like the newsletter you did." I walked away, baffled like that's not what the Lord meant. No one knew I was to be an author and academic researcher with published works. Reader, have you noticed the Lord was also using laypeople to confirm His plan for my life? 1st Corinthians 14:31 declares that all should be allowed to prophesy, not just the leader, that all may learn and be comforted. See, when the Lord has something for you to do, few will know about it. You just have to follow the Lord.

Following the Lord does not imply you don't love your family. Following the Lord does not mean you are angry with someone. And it does not mean you are disobeying Church authority. I had family members who thought I was mad at them because I could no longer see them. It is plain and simple: I must be about my Father's business. I think about and pray for my family daily, often laughing about how things used to be. But, I must be about my Father's business.

I had to forgive numerous people; they said and did some awful things because they did not understand why the Lord put me in my mother's womb. I'm thankful for the experience since it helped me to grow up. Now, I have more understanding and lasting contentment with what the Lord is doing. Each day He reveals more of His plan, and each day I'm empowered to agree and walk in His plan for my life. Forgiveness is the key to healing, and humility is essential to getting understanding from the Lord.

Reader, pray this prayer with me:

Abba, Father, in the name of Jesus Christ of Nazareth, give me the strength to obey the Holy Spirit and follow You and accept Your plan for my life. Do what You have to do to fulfill Your will in my life, in Jesus' name. Amen.

CHAPTER THIRTEEN

YOUR LEADER CAN'T PROMOTE YOU

"And how shall they preach, except they be sent? as it is written, How beautiful are the feet of them that preach the gospel of peace, and bring glad tidings of good things!"

Romans 10:15

What I'm about to explain is only written for your understanding. It is not to boast, for we only boast in the Lord. I know a person who gave their life to Jesus and later found out they had a calling on their life. After giving their life to Jesus, they immediately started faithfully attending the ministry where the Lord sent them. As with many saints, they had a rocky start in their walk with the Lord due to the fleshly struggles believers go through when they come out of darkness into the Lord's marvelous light. However, the person continued to press their way until they became stable in their walk with the Lord.

Shortly after the person gave their life to Jesus, the Church's Elder was sent to a new assignment, and another Elder took over. After the first Elder left, everyone stopped attending services except for the new saint. The saint continued to participate in Church faithfully, even when the new Elder of the Church did not show to open the doors. There were times when the saint would wait in their car for hours, and the Elder never showed. Then the Lord told the new Elder of the ministry to make sure he showed up for service for the new saint's sake. So, a typical Church service included the Elder, his family, and the new saint.

As time went on, the faithful saint was growing in the Lord; the Lord added souls to the Church, and the house of God began to prosper. Now mind you, the Church building where they had ministry was shared by several ministries, and none took the initiative to clean. So, the faithful saint began to clean the building alone without being told, including the regularly disgusting bathrooms and kitchen. Some of the new members would tease the faithful saint when they saw them cleaning the bathroom. They would say, "You're doing a great job there. That job fits you."

Then the leader announced that a promotion ceremony would take place in three months for those called to be Ministers. At the time, the faithful saint did not know what type of promotion ceremony of which the leader spoke. However, they dove into the Word of God daily, preparing for ministry. As time progressed, the day came when the leader promoted seven people to be Ministers with no specific capacity. Then the Elder said, "This is the last person I will be promoting today." The person anxiously awaited the calling of their name. However, someone else was chosen. The saint who was faithful to the Lord when no one else was faithful did not get a promotion. Instead, those who teased the faithful saint received a promotion, and those new Ministers did not even know the Word of God.

After he promoted the last person, the faithful saint said within themselves, "I'm leaving this place, and I'm never ever coming back." At that particular time, the leader spoke, "I need to see so-and-so in the baptismal room." The faithful saint and the leader went to the baptismal room. The Lord told the leader to tell the faithful saint, *"Make sure you don't leave. I have something for you, but I need you to stay here and endure, and get what I have for you."* At that moment, the faithful saint felt like God had stuck His hand through their chest, pulled their heart out, and looked at it while it was beating. That's the immense hurt the person felt because they did not understand it was not man promoting, but God who chose the vessels for promotion.

Furthermore, to add insult to injury, the seven people who received promotions would still see the person downstairs mopping floors, cleaning the kitchen and restroom facilities. They all continued to make comments, "I told you that you had the right position. That's all you're good for." And that faithful saint began to wear immense hurt on their shoulders like a king wearing a long black flowing robe that dragged the floor. They dragged their injury around with them to the point where it showed on their face.

Moreover, the leadership changed for the third time, and it was still the same; there was no promotion. There was nothing but more humiliation and ridicule, and this time even the leader began to insult the faithful saint. Years went by, and the Lord told the faithful saint to let the third leader know they had a calling to be a Minister. The leader responded, "Well, give me two or three months, and I will get back to you." After three months, the faithful saint received a promotion as an attendant and not a ministerial position. It seemed like the beginning of the end. Then the Lord began to speak to that faithful saint more avidly.

However, the faithful saint did not realize the Lord had been working with them the whole time. The Lord started them out as a Teacher, teaching Sunday school to children aged two to ten. Then they progressed to fourteen-year-olds, ending at seventeen-year-olds. Finally, they ministered to all of the youth. Next, the Lord made them a Pastor and assigned them to teach the Word of God and care for a particular group of souls. Then the Lord had them operating as an Evangelist, appointing them to bring the Gospel message to those at their workplace.

As an Evangelist, the Lord commanded them to stand on the street corner and evangelize morning, noon, and night through nice sunny days to bitter cold and rainy days. Then they heard the Lord tell them they had a calling to a Prophetic Office, and the saint did not respond. Then the Lord repeated it on the third day, *"Didn't I tell you I have called you to a Prophetic Office?"* Again, the saint did not answer because they were not trying to be anything in the Lord. It was just confusing because the Lord was saying one thing, and the leaders were saying another. Despite what the Lord said, the faithful saint never received a promotion to a ministerial position by humans, but the Lord was sovereignly using that faithful saint how He saw fit.

Later, the people who previously taunted the faithful saint began to see a positive change in them, and two of those people started to respect them as a Prophetic Officer. They said, "I knew there was something different about you. I did not know what it was then, but I know what it is now." The Lord would often use them at work to minister, and many of their co-workers understood they had a Prophetic Officer in their midst. Then things began to take flight, and the faithful saint's life changed. Not only did their understanding increase, their healing came forth because they realized it was God who promoted people and not man.

With that said, some callings are sovereign, meaning some people will be sovereignly placed in their offices by the Lord. All believers must understand, not every spiritual leader is appropriately equipped or called of God to put saints in their offices. I was in a Church that had no Five-Fold officers over the Church, so they could not anoint me into the offices of Evangelist or Prophetess. All the Five-Fold offices are higher offices than Elders, Bishops, or even Archbishops. It takes a Prophet or Apostle by instruction from the Holy Ghost to place four of the Five-Fold officers into their offices. Only the Lord Jesus Christ has the authority to set a man into the office of an Apostle. A Prophet or another Apostle cannot put an Apostle in his office.

Didn't Jesus choose Himself twelve men Apostles? Well, the way He selected Apostles back then is the way He chooses Apostles today. For example, in the Bible, the Lord Jesus chose Paul to be His Apostle. That is how He chooses Apostles in this day and age. It has nothing to do with humans. Believe me, I know, because the Lord Jesus Christ told my husband on various occasions, he is His Apostle, and gave him the Scripture in Matthew 10:1-20. After my husband read the verses, the Lord said, *"That's what you are to Me."* The Lord also showed my husband many supernatural events as a witness of His resurrection. He has seen Jesus on numerous occasions. After that, the Lord confirmed to my husband that he is the Lord's Apostle Prophet. Furthermore, the Lord gave me a dream that my husband is a man likened to Moses.

Some people are hurting and are angry with a Church leader because the leader did not recognize their calling to ministry. When people get mad because things are not going how they think they should go, the adversary provokes them to anger. My husband taught me long ago that believers do not realize that when they speak out of their mouths, doors are opened for the adversary to know precisely where they are spiritually. But if they would *submit* themselves *to God* and *resist the devil*, then *the devil would flee* from them, James 4:7. But if they do not know the Scriptures, how can they operate in something they do not know. Preventing the adversary from getting a foothold in our lives is one reason the Lord requires us to read the Bible. Since you now know it is the adversary making you angry, you need to let the anger go. Besides, most leaders do not have the authority to anoint you into your office for several reasons.

Firstly, your calling is to a higher office than the leader's office where you are attending Church. Secondly, the Lord has not revealed to the leader you have a calling. Thirdly, it is not for your

305

spiritual leader to know your work is more significant than their work, lest they start saying, you will never be greater than me, which leads to other hurtful things. Fourthly, if you will be more anointed than the leader, he cannot train you in all the areas you need training. Fifthly, most leaders do not understand the Five-Fold offices. A lot of people think being gifted puts them in a Five-Fold office. It's not the gift; it's the authority that goes with an office. Authority can only be given and recognized by the Lord Jesus Christ.

Sixthly, many Elders, Bishops, and Pastors do not understand many people in their ministry have callings to Five-Fold offices. It is not like it used to be in the previous days when leaders were few and far between. The Lord said in Joel 2:28-29, *"And it shall come to pass afterward, that I will pour out my spirit upon all flesh; and your sons and your daughters shall prophesy, your old men shall dream dreams, your young men shall see visions: And also upon the servants and upon the handmaids in those days will I pour out my spirit."* That outpouring includes callings and anointings for offices, not just gifts of the Spirit.

Seventhly, many who are in the Offices of Deacon, Elder, and Bishop should be in Five-Fold offices. Unfortunately, some forced their way into those lower offices, or men put them in those offices, yet it was never the plan of the Lord. Years ago, the Lord showed me in a dream a Pastor who became a Bishop, but the Lord never called him to be a Bishop. The Lord had a greater purpose for his life. However, because it was popular to be called a Bishop, the person coveted the Office. After much searching to find someone to anoint him into the Bishop's office, all the doors were closed, yet the person did not realize it was the Lord. He thought it was the devil blocking his blessing to become a Bishop. He assumed it would be a promotion because a Bishop can oversee more than one ministry, but instead, it was a demotion.

Anyway, the person refused to accept defeat, so as a last resort, he finally found a Bishop who reluctantly held the ceremony and placed him in the Office of Bishop. The Lord gave him over to his desires, yet it was not the Lord's original plan. At first, the person seemed to prosper because of becoming a Bishop, but over time the person's ministry began to diminish and never came to full fruition. I had a second dream that they were standing amid the congregation, and their authority began to diminish more and more. Then I had a third dream that their ministry was stagnated because they refused to hear several vessels the Lord sent to correct them. Trying to make yourself something the Lord didn't call you to will have far-reaching consequences for you and your ministry.

Reader, you must understand, Bishops are Senior Elders who oversee Churches run by Elders and Deacons until the Lord appoints a Shepherd (Pastor). A Pastor is a Five-Fold Office according to Ephesians 4:11. A Bishop is a senior Elder, which is an Office lower than a Pastor. Also, an Archbishop is an overseer of Bishops. The Deacon, Elder, Bishop, and Archbishop are supporting offices for Five-Fold Officers, according to Acts 6:1-4, 1st Timothy 3:1-15, Titus 1:5, and 1st Corinthians 12:28. Consider Apostle Paul was instructing Timothy and Titus, not the other way around, yet that's another book.

Finally, your leader can't promote you because the leader will not understand or relate to those things the Lord will have you doing. For example, misunderstandings are widespread concerning those called of the Lord. Since few understand the charge of Five-Fold Officers, those called to lead in these offices will baffle many. Just know this: the Lord said *there is a lot of error in the Body of Christ because the people who are calling themselves Apostles are not true Apostles.*

One vital sign of a true Apostle of the Lord Jesus Christ is establishing and understanding true Bible doctrine, and I mean the whole Canon. That understanding of Scripture will be imparted to true Apostles by the Lord Jesus Christ when they stand in His presence to receive their charge. Yes, the office will have signs following, yet so do the other offices because the power of the Holy Ghost shall be on the lives of all true believers, just in different measures. The other significant sign is the training and sending forth of Five-Fold Officers into the Earth to do the will of God. And true Apostles will not have man-made requirements to meet your calling. True Apostles love to see Churches planted without humans trying to take credit for what the Lord is doing.

Consider, many Holy Ghost filled Churches are led by a Five-Fold Officer or Bishop. Unfortunately, some of these leaders think everyone sitting under their leadership is called to be laity or lay leadership. However, in truth, many of those were born to lead ministries and watch for souls. The Lord told me to share this dream from years ago. When I was a young believer, I saw the pictures of several Elders and their wives on Church programs, similar to the one used in the Church we all attended. Each couple had their own ministry program with a picture of each couple in the upper left corner of the first page. The ministry programs had the names of different ministries. Each program also had a short biography on the couple and the service schedule for the day. I awoke and smiled at what the Lord had shown. I knew some promotions were coming, and many would soon leave to start ministries.

Soon after I had that dream, the same Elders were all promoted to Pastors except two. One who did not receive a promotion pleaded his case to no avail. It was shared with the congregation that the Lord said it was not time, yet the Elder said the Lord told him it was time. What seemed like a contradiction was no contradiction at all; both were hearing from the Lord. Apparently, the Lord did not desire that particular leader to promote him. He had something else for him. I knew none of the people personally, nor did I know when everything was supposed to occur. I just know that the Lord showed me many things before they happened, even making His will known unto me as He did the spiritual leader. Now, I understand that I was chosen to be a Prophetess. The Lord has checks and balances. It takes humility to serve the Lord.

The second Elder who was not promoted was so faithful he continued to wait on the Lord, even though the Lord already saw him as a Pastor. To confirm his promotion the Lord sent a visiting Prophet who had no idea about him and his perplexing situation. While ministering, the Prophet began to ask for him by name, calling him

Pastor so and so. He was not even in the sanctuary. He was faithfully working somewhere else in the building. Once he came into the sanctuary, the Lord told him that he was His Pastor. Long story short, after the Prophet finished ministering, the Leader immediately began to say the Pastor could not be called a Pastor until the Lord cleared it with the leader first. I was sitting there excited that the Lord showed me he was already a Pastor. It does not matter what man says because the Lord told me, *"Man is just a puppet on a string."* The Lord will always use man to show us what we will do; can you obey the Lord through adversity? We will be tested and tried concerning our obedience to the Lord and what He requires of us.

After the promotion ceremony, none of the Pastors left the Church to start the Lord's work, which was baffling to me. Was it because they were promoted to a position higher than the one doing the promotion? That type of confusion will cause trouble for the one promoted. If you start in error, you will end in error if the Lord does not have mercy. When the Lord has chosen you for something, not everyone will agree with the Lord's plan. You just have to step out in faith when it is time. Obey the Lord before the window the Lord has set closes, and remember man cannot make you something the LORD did not call or choose you to be.

The clarification comes by considering 80 to 90% of all Churches have Deacons, Elders, Bishops, or Pastors as leaders. Most organizations do not operate in Five-Fold offices. Many do not even believe in the indwelling of the Holy Ghost. And if you find a few who do move by the Holy Ghost, they will not be able to anoint you into your office. Therefore, those called to Five-Fold offices may feel hopeless because nobody can help them if they are sitting under leadership who do not understand their place in the Body of Christ. And believe me, all Churches are called to at least understand the Five-Fold Offices.

It is a serious matter if you belong to an organization that does not believe in the indwelling of the Holy Ghost. Romans 8:9 declares, *"But ye are not in the flesh, but in the Spirit, if so be that the Spirit of God dwell in you. Now if any man have not the Spirit of Christ, he is none of his."* If you have the Holy Ghost, there will be evidence of His presence living inside of you. Commonly, those who have the Holy Ghost will speak in unknown tongues (Acts 2:4) or prophesy (Joel 2:28-29). According to 1st John chapter 4, the person will continually confess, *"Jesus Christ is come in the flesh* (verses 2-3), and *Jesus is the Son of God"* (verses 13-15). And 1st Corinthians 12:3 declares, *"Wherefore I give you to understand, that no man speaking by the Spirit of God calleth Jesus accursed: and that no man can say that Jesus is the Lord, but by the Holy Ghost."*

If you do not have the Holy Spirit living inside you, you do not belong to Jesus. Meaning, you need to follow the instructions laid out by Apostle Peter in Acts 2:38, *"Then Peter said unto them, Repent, and be baptized every one of you in the name of Jesus Christ for the remission of sins, and ye shall receive the gift of the Holy Ghost."* I have asked a lot of people who said they believe in Jesus Christ if they had received the Holy Ghost since they believed, and their response to me was always: "I think so; I believe I do, or I would like to believe I do."

Acts 19:2-7 declares, *"He said unto them, Have ye received the Holy Ghost since ye believed? And they said unto him, We have not so much as heard whether there be any Holy Ghost. And he said unto them, Unto what then were ye baptized? And they said, Unto John's baptism. Then said Paul, John verily baptized with the baptism of repentance, saying unto the people, that they should believe on him which should come after him, that is, on Christ Jesus. When they heard this, they were baptized in the name of the Lord Jesus. And when Paul had laid his hands upon them, the Holy Ghost came on*

313

them; and they spake with tongues, and prophesied. And all the men were about twelve."

When you have the Holy Ghost, you know it. He is like nothing else you have ever experienced. He walks with you, and He talks to you daily. He strengthens and preserves you and your relationship with the Lord Jesus and God the Father. He is the one who gives wisdom. He is the Lord God living inside of you. It is by the Holy Spirit we pray, fast, and understand the Word of God. He is part of the Trinity. You need Him.

When I gave my life to Jesus, I repented of my sins during an evening service, and the same night they baptized me in water in the name of the Lord Jesus Christ. Immediately following my water baptism, the salvation team worked with me until nearly midnight to receive the gift of the Holy Spirit with the evidence of speaking in tongues. I doubted what was happening, so the Holy Ghost could not come in and dwell inside me.

I felt I was okay because I repented, and they baptized me in water. I felt so light and free that I wondered why I needed tongues. My confession had changed, and I freely confessed Jesus Christ as Lord. Yes, by the Spirit of the Lord, I confessed my sins, yet it was not enough to strengthen me for a long walk with Jesus. I needed the power of God living on the inside of me in a greater measure. At the end of the evening, one of the Church Mothers gave me a book to read titled *Why Tongues* by Kenneth E. Hagin. She told me we would try again after I read the book. I read the book as soon as I got home and knew I needed tongues. Nine days after I repented of my sins, I received the indwelling of the Holy Ghost with the gift of tongues.

Having the Holy Spirit of God is vital to our walk in the Lord. During the nine days before receiving the indwelling of the Holy Spirit, I could not understand the Bible. Although I did not understand, I still tried to read it daily to no avail. It is only by the indwelling of the Holy Ghost that we can operate in the things of God. It is through the Holy Spirit that we follow the leading and guidance of the Lord. It is by the Holy Ghost that we will receive the Kingdom of Heaven.

Oh! When I received the Holy Ghost, a whole new world opened to me. I started speaking in an unknown tongue and didn't desire to stop speaking because I did not desire the gift of utterance by the Holy Ghost to cease. Immediately, when the Holy Ghost came, a spirit of intelligence fled. I was empowered to stop cussing, fussing, fornicating, and masturbating. I immediately stopped. My mind began a renewal process. Finally, I could understand the Bible and have now read it too many times for me to count. I still love reading it daily. You see, the Holy Ghost keeps me strengthened and encouraged on this long journey with Jesus. The Holy Ghost continually builds my character.

You need to have evidence you have the Holy Ghost. To just think so is not enough. It is like a person who has to take a long journey in a gasoline-powered vehicle that has a broken gas gauge; the driver is not sure how much gasoline is in the car, and they are passing the last gas station for 50 miles. I can hear the driver saying, I think I have a full tank. No! We need to pull over and make sure we have a full tank of gas. There needs to be evidence. When the gauge no longer works, the only way to know is to pull into a refueling station and attempt to top off your tank.

When the Lord calls you out and instructs you to come forth, the Holy Ghost helps you follow the Lord. The Lord is the One who called you, so He is the only One who can assist you in what He has called you to do. You must obey the Lord and go where He called you to be. If the Lord sends you to a Five-Fold ministry, then you are called to a Five-Fold office.

The Lord told me to share with you another thing that happened when He called me forth to ministry. He not only told me to prepare for ministry, but he showed me a dream. In the dream, I entered the Church sanctuary. All the leaders usually sat on the front row across the entire sanctuary, and the seats were always filled. On this particular day, several seats were open, and I walked to the chair that was appointed for me. Another sister did the same thing, sitting next to me. While we were sitting there, the other seats filled up with none left open. Then someone walked up to us and started yelling, "Get out of my seat." We replied, "We are not going anywhere, and you can't make us get up. She continued her demands. We continued to sit there saying nothing. She yelled, "If you don't get up, I'm going to make you." I thought, just don't touch me. Then the person next to me said, I think I'm going sit in the back. I said, "You don't have to." The other woman continued yelling, and the person next to me picked up her belongings, walked away, and took a seat in the back of the sanctuary. The other woman immediately sat down with an attitude.

When I awoke, I knew it meant that we were called to leadership in the Lord's Kingdom, but the promotion would not come without a fight. We had to stand our ground. When I told the other person about my dream, she said it had already happened. She gave up her opportunity because other people had a problem with her; they made things difficult. I asked her why she cared what others thought?

I also told her that she should only care about what the Lord thinks, and she shrugged her shoulders. I thought, well Lord, I desire to be all you have chosen me to be. So far, He has blessed me to take a stand for Him. Reader, now that you understand, you should realize that being angry with the leader is useless since he could not place you in a Five-Fold office even if he desired. The Lord decides who He is choosing.

I will make the last point for those who are angry because the Lord did not call them to serve in a ministerial office. The bottom line is no one can make themselves a Minister. The Lord must choose you. John 15:16 explains, *"Ye have not chosen me, but I have chosen you, and ordained you, that ye should go and bring forth fruit, and that your fruit should remain: that whatsoever ye shall ask of the Father in my name, he may give it you."*

The only one who calls, chooses, equips, and sends is the Lord Jesus Christ! Romans 10:15 is clear, *"And how shall they preach, except they be sent? as it is written, How beautiful are the feet of them that preach the gospel of peace, and bring glad tidings of good things!"* If the Lord did not call you to preach, it does not mean you do not have a purpose. If the Lord called you out of the world, He has a plan for you, and it is not to be a pew warmer. Seek the Lord instead of getting angry, and Jesus will reveal His perfect design for your life. Once He makes His plan known, obey and follow Him.

Reader, pray this prayer with me:

Abba, Father, in the name of Jesus Christ of Nazareth, forgive me for being angry with my spiritual leader for not promoting me. I know You are the only one who calls and chooses leaders. The Bible declares in Psalm 75:6-7 promotion does not come from the east, nor the west, nor from the south, but from You Lord who puts down one and sets up another. Show me Your will for my life, and I will follow. If You called me to leadership, help me to serve where you have placed me. Then, when the appointed time is upon me, open a door so I can step into what You are calling me to. Please give me the strength to obey Your command to step out into leadership. If there is an Apostle or Prophet, who will train and anoint me into my office, show me Lord, and order my steps to bring me into their presence, in Jesus' name. Amen.

CHAPTER FOURTEEN

THE SEGREGATED CHURCH

"And he taught, saying unto them, Is it not written, My house shall be called of all nations the house of prayer? but ye have made it a den of thieves."

Mark 11:17

"For the time is come that judgment must begin at the house of God: and if it first begin at us, what shall the end be of them that obey not the gospel of God" (1st Peter 4:17)? What more pain can someone experience than the Lord sending them to a Church, and it is made clear they are unwelcome by the leaders or those in the congregation because they are of a different race, nationality, denomination, or political association?

Unfortunately, some in the Church promote doctrines that oppress and exclude other races and nationalities from fellowshipping with the saints. Instead of teaching the law of love, they encourage hatred. They refuse to let go of the sins of our forefathers, and believe me, they all sinned. Apostle Paul admonished, *"Beware lest any man spoil you through philosophy and vain deceit, after the tradition of men, after the rudiments of the world, and not after Christ"* (Colossians 2:8). No one stops to consider what is going on in the Churches today. No one pauses to ask the Lord how He sees things. I asked the Lord how He sees the Critical Race Theory movement. He immediately responded: *". . . forgetting those things which are behind, and reaching forth unto those things which are before, I press toward the mark for the prize of the high calling of God in Christ Jesus.*" What? The Lord is saying, *"Let it go."* Besides, it will mean nothing when it is all said and done if people don't know Jesus Christ as Lord and Saviour. All of this world's system will come to an end (2nd Peter 3:10).

I have visited many Churches in America, large and small, and my husband has visited many Churches in America and several in Europe. All were unofficially segregated, except a few in Europe. Galatians 3:26-29 declares, *"For ye are all the children of God by faith in Christ Jesus. For as many of you as have been baptized into Christ have put on Christ. There is neither Jew nor Greek, there is neither bond nor free, there is neither male nor female: for ye are all one in Christ Jesus. And if ye be Christ's, then are ye Abraham's seed, and heirs according to the promise."*

Faith in Jesus Christ is supposed to unite us, not tear us apart. Faith connects our homes, communities, and nation. But we have to allow faith in Jesus to reign and not our economic and social status. When we are connected, we are unified. In unity, there is power, love, and hope. A unified Church is stronger than a Church divided. The enemy will lose all influence over the saints when we are unified in love. *"Beloved, let us love one another: for love is of God; and every*

324

one that loveth is born of God, and knoweth God. He that loveth not knoweth not God; for God is love. In this was manifested the love of God toward us, because that God sent his only begotten Son into the world, that we might live through him. Herein is love, not that we loved God, but that he loved us, and sent his Son to be the propitiation for our sins" (1ˢᵗ John 4:7-10).

How can we hope to heal as a nation of people if we do not love one another? By love, the world identifies the Church as the Lord's disciples. No matter what country you live in, if you believe in the Lord Jesus Christ, you are a member of a united Body of believers. You are not a member of a denomination, political association, or racial group. You are united by the Holy Spirit of God, which dwells in you, into the Body of Christ. The Lord told me, *"The Body of Christ is the most powerful nation in the Earth, not America and not Israel." The reason you and your husband are not concerned about politics is because I AM your King."* He also said, *"The reason I defend Israel as a nation is for my namesake."*

There is a new covenant that includes Gentiles and Jews (Romans 3:29 and Revelation 5:9), and love is the attribute that shows us and the world that the Holy Ghost reigns in the believer's life. The Bible is clear, *"A new commandment I give unto you, That ye love one another; as I have loved you, that ye also love one another. By this shall all men know that ye are my disciples, if ye have love one to another"* (John 13:34-35).

Furthermore, Ezekiel 18:4 declares, *"Behold, all souls are mine; as the soul of the father, so also the soul of the son is mine: . . ."* If nothing else, those who claim to be Christians should love all men's souls, which have no color or nationality. We are citizens in Heaven, first and foremost (Hebrews 11:13 f-only). And if we are citizens, we need to conduct ourselves like citizens of the Kingdom of GOD.

Apostle Paul was no stranger to hatred and persecution. He gave sound counsel concerning what we should do when faced with persecution. Paul said, *"Bless them which persecute you: bless, and curse not. Rejoice with them that do rejoice, and weep with them that weep. Be of the same mind one toward another. Mind not high things, but condescend to men of low estate. Be not wise in your own conceits. Recompense to no man evil for evil. Provide things honest in the sight of all men. If it be possible, as much as lieth in you, live peaceably with all men. Dearly beloved, avenge not yourselves, but rather give place unto wrath: for it is written, Vengeance is mine; I* will repay, saith the Lord. Therefore if thine enemy hunger, feed him; if he thirst, give him drink: for in so doing thou shalt heap coals of fire on his head. Be not overcome of evil, but overcome evil with good" (Romans 12:14-21).

Even the physician and historian Luke recorded Jesus saying, *"But I say unto you which hear, Love your enemies, do good to them which hate you, Bless them that curse you, and pray for them which despitefully use you. And unto him that smiteth thee on the one cheek offer also the other; and him that taketh away thy cloke forbid not to take thy coat also. Give to every man that asketh of thee; and of him that taketh away thy goods ask them not again. And as ye would that men should do to you, do ye also to them likewise. For if ye love them which love you, what thank have ye? for sinners also love those that love them. And if ye do good to them which do good to you, what thank have ye? for sinners also do even the same. And if ye lend to them of whom ye hope to receive, what thank have ye? for sinners also lend to sinners, to receive as much again. But love ye your enemies, and do good, and lend, hoping for nothing again; and your reward shall be great, and ye shall be the children of the Highest: for he is kind unto the unthankful and to the evil. Be ye therefore merciful, as your Father also is merciful. Judge not, and ye shall not be judged: condemn not, and ye shall not be condemned: forgive, and ye shall be forgiven:"* (Luke 6:27-37).

More importantly, Jesus, our Lord, being the most righteous of all men, suffered the ultimate persecution and was put to death. Amid His trial, when everyone derided Him, He held steadfast to His teachings. *"Ye have heard that it hath been said, Thou shalt love thy neighbour, and hate thine enemy. But I say unto you, Love your enemies, bless them that curse you, do good to them that hate you, and pray for them which despitefully use you, and persecute you; That ye may be the children of your Father which is in heaven: for he maketh his sun to rise on the evil and on the good, and sendeth rain on the just and on the unjust. For if ye love them which love you, what reward have ye? do not even the publicans the same? And if ye salute your brethren only, what do ye more than others? do not even the publicans so? Be ye therefore perfect, even as your Father which is in heaven is perfect"* (Matthew 5:43-48).

Jesus and Paul both instructed us to do good to those who do us wrong. I know it is hard to accept the Lord's doctrine, especially with all the people in this world who operate in hatred. But, I do good to others because I genuinely love souls. I also do it to please the

328

Lord, and I do it to keep evil from making my heart dark. So, I always endeavor to overcome evil with a holy conversation and deeds, no matter how it hurts. I choose to do what I expect others to do to me in the same situation. No matter what everyone else is doing, I choose to do the right thing in the eyes of the Lord!

When someone is mistreating me, I pray for them. It is a neutral place that allows the Lord's will to come forth. If the Lord desires to judge that person for their deeds, then so be it. If He has something else planned, it is not my concern what He chooses to do with someone else. Amen. If the Lord sends you to a Church and you experience mistreatment, forgive quickly, lest you suffer the consequences of unforgivingness. Never leave a Church because someone hurt your feelings. Stay because it pleases Jesus when you stay where He placed you. Jesus gave us the perfect example while at the height of His persecution: *". . . Father, forgive them; for they know not what they do . . ."* (Luke 23:34 b-d only). Note, just because you forgive someone, it does not mean the Father has forgiven them. Therefore, Jesus asked God the Father to forgive them because Jesus had already forgiven them. Yet, again, the world teaches retaliation and revenge. Romans 12:2 warns, *"And be not conformed to this world: but be ye transformed by the renewing of your mind, that ye may prove what is that good, and acceptable, and perfect will of God.”*

I know you have deep hurt due to the racial tension in the Church and country, but your pain stems from a lack of understanding. I know people do not believe in the Bible anymore, but God's Word will remain true forever. Jesus Christ is the Word of God. You cannot say you believe in Him and ignore His Word. I am persuaded that *Jesus, even Yeshua, is the Messiah, and He is Lord.* The Bible exclaims: *"Jesus saith unto him, I am the way, the truth, and the life: no man cometh unto the Father, but by me"* (John 14:6). If you fully believe in the Word of God, then you have to accept the Lord's counsel to love and forgive.

I know many people who have unforgivingness in their hearts, and they refuse to get rid of that unforgivingness. Collectively, if millions operate in unforgivingness, it would negatively affect the whole nation. You have to see yourself as that one righteous person that can affect the entire country's wellbeing. The Lord uses nature to destroy lands every year, whether by fire, earthquake, volcanoes, storms, floods, drought, or famine (Genesis 7:11-24 and 19:24-25). However, if one righteous person dwells in the land and an Apostle, Prophet or Prophetess intercedes on behalf of the nation, the Lord may deter judgment; or at least He will rescue the righteous (Genesis 18:23-33). For that reason, I strive daily to position myself to be that one who can intercede for souls in the land. Yet, if I hate on people, the Lord will not hear my prayers. No matter what people think, the condition of your heart is what matters. Only the Lord knows your true intention, so strive to keep your heart right before Him.

From nation to nation, we are living in tumultuous times. He is a God who sees and knows everything (Proverbs 15:3 and 1st John 3:20). The whole world is in an uproar over things that are not in man's control. Most people do not understand that God controls everything that happens on the Earth, and He has a purpose for everything He orchestrates. We like to say He allows things because it is easier to swallow, comprehend, and process through our finite minds. But, He actually has a hand in everything that happens. He chooses all the players in His Divine design.

Real change comes by way of adversity. If you desire change, he will put you through the fire. *"See now that I, even I, am he, and there is no god with me: I kill, and I make alive; I wound, and I heal: neither is there any that can deliver out of my hand"* (Deuteronomy 32:39). Everything belongs to the Lord, and He controls who gets wealth and who doesn't. *"THE earth is the LORD's, and the fulness thereof; the world, and they that dwell therein"* (Psalms 24:1). *"The silver is mine, and the gold is mine, saith the LORD of hosts"* (Haggai 2:8). *"For every beast of the forest is mine, and the cattle upon a thousand hills. I know all the fowls of the mountains: and the wild beasts of the field are mine. If I were hungry, I would not tell thee: for the world is mine, and the fulness thereof"* (Psalm 50:10-12).

The Lord instructed me to tell you He is in control of who gets what land. The Lord gave the Canaanite's land to Abram and His descendants (Genesis 12:1-7). And when the Israelites displeased Him, He removed them from their land (Jeremiah 13:19). When they repented, the Lord gave the land back to them. *"But, The LORD liveth, that brought up the children of Israel from the land of the north, and from all the lands whither he had driven them: and I will bring them again into their land that I gave unto their fathers"* (Jeremiah 16:15). Reader, please understand: *". . . the most High ruleth in the kingdom of men, and giveth it to whomsoever he will"* (Daniel 4:32 e-f only). *"John answered and said, A man can receive nothing, except it be given him from heaven"* (John 3:27).

The Lord Jesus is in control of where we live (Acts 17:26). He is the one who gives *knowledge of witty inventions* (Proverbs 8:12). And He is the one who gives *power to get wealth* (Deuteronomy

8:18). The Lord would not have us fighting over land, money, power, religion, or politics. Jesus is not a republican, democrat, independent, capitalist, fascists, communist, socialist, or any other such thing. And He does not ascribe to a particular religious denomination. If you have the Holy Spirit, then you belong to Him (Romans 8:9). He is the one who decides everything.

It is impossible to erase what happened to the Native Americans, Hispanics, Africans, Jews, and Asians in this world. Who can bring back all the souls lost during the Holocaust? No amount of money can appease races of people who have experienced that level of trauma. No words can explain it, and the truth that the Lord was in control is too painful for many to bear. No, we cannot change the past, but we can forgive. However, heinous, I have come to terms with the cruelty done to my fore-parents only because I know the Lord was in control. If you don't believe the Lord is in control of what happens to you amid mistreatment, look at the narratives of slaves like Olaudah Equiano (a.k.a. Gustavus Vassa), Frederick Douglass, and Harriet Tubman. All these slaves and many more obtained favor from the Lord. There are countless testimonials of how the Lord was actively working in the lives of the slaves and moving on their behalf and Caucasians took up their cause.

Surrendering your life to the Lord Jesus Christ is the only way to heal the hearts of man. It is time to stop fighting and saying they stole our land. They enslaved us. They owe us. I am telling you reparations can only come from the Lord. Cry out to the Lord if you desire reparations. If He grants it, Amen! And if He does not, Amen! Let it go! Additionally, if you feel the Europeans stole your land, understand, the Lord is the one who gave away your land, and He does not need a reason. The land belongs to the Lord.

The Lord is the one who allowed the enslavement of many, and when He said, *"It is enough!"* He set the people free. Unfortunately, many people in the world, besides Africans and Jews, have been taken captive by men. Robert Davis, an Ohio State University professor, reported many American seaman, British, European Christians, French, Italians, Portuguese, and Spaniards were enslaved in various numbers (Grabmeier, 2004). And many more of all creeds are persecuted daily.

Furthermore, Chinese and Korean women were also enslaved and sexually exploited (Blakemore, 2019). Unfortunately, today, these types of atrocities are still happening to many of all nationalities. Slavery is not a thing isolated to one group. It is a great evil in the Earth rooted in greed, not skin color, gender, or religion. It is about money and opportunity. Listen, land is money! How? The land has riches in it, which can be unearthed. And somebody figured humans were worth money too, in more ways than one. *"But they that will be rich fall into temptation and a snare, and into many foolish and hurtful lusts, which drown men in destruction and perdition. For the love of money is the root of all evil: which while some coveted after, they have erred from the faith, and pierced themselves through with many sorrows"* (1st Timothy 6:9-10). And many nations of people allowed the devil to wreak havoc in their lives when that nation did not serve the Lord God who created them. *"Neither give place to the devil"* (Ephesians 4:27).

Those who exploit humans for any reason are called menstealers in the Bible, and the Lord will judge them. That is the reason the Lord said, *". . . the law is not made for a righteous man, but for the lawless and disobedient, for the ungodly and for sinners, for unholy and profane, for murderers of fathers and murderers of mothers, for manslayers, . . . for menstealers, for liars, . . .* (1st Timothy 1:9-10). Thus, the Bible describes menstealers as unrighteous, lawless, disobedient, and having ways contrary to sound doctrine. What does any of this have to do with the Church? Many say they believe in Jesus and claim to be serving Him, yet they won't forgive these atrocities.

However, if we do not forgive all of the atrocities committed against us as a people and as humans, the enemy will have succeeded in keeping us from moving forward. You do not have to be angry to fight. Actually, when you become angry during a fight, you lose. And retaliation only brings more pain. I would rather obey the Scriptures whether other people think it is appropriate or not. I would rather pray and ask the Lord for what I desire instead of asking man. You must understand you are fighting a principality. You can only fight a principality through prayer and fasting in the name of the Lord Jesus Christ. Only the Lord has the power to defeat a principality. And He has delegated authority to those in the Church to tear down whatever seeks to recapture us. We all have a responsibility to pray and fight in the spirit realm. Whatever affects other families affects us all. If you do not assist the saints in praying against the controlling spiritual authority that we all battle, you will be a partaker in the atrocities the principality continues to commit.

Jesus said *a house or country divided against itself cannot stand, but has an end* (Mark 3:24-26). That is why Christians seem to be weak in fighting against the wiles of the devil. Instead of standing firm in fighting the forces of evil driving the racial divide, many enjoy the privileges afforded by others' plight. We have to be willing to confront racial issues within our hearts if we are to move forward in the Lord. And those who have experienced racial mistreatment must find healing through forgiveness and teach others how to go through the process with a forgiving spirit. Someone who has a forgiving spirit will quickly forgive because they understand human nature is flawed and subject to err.

Nevertheless, if you refuse to forgive, you will pollute others with your false doctrine. If that is not true, then why is the Body of Christ still segregated? Why do you only feel comfortable attending Church with people who behave, think, look, and talk like you? And why is there friction and strife amongst Church members when the Lord brings in families who are different from the majority group? Finally, why do some spiritual leaders promote segregation? I'll tell you why: hatred and unforgivingness.

I remember someone of another race who came to our ministry. We were excited because years earlier, my husband saw a vision of us standing, wearing all white, holding a multicolored patchwork baby. Since his ministry started in Europe, he knew the Lord was telling him we would have a Church of diverse people. So shortly before they began attending services, my husband prayed within himself and asked the Lord, "If it is your will for me to continue the ministry, send in someone who is of another race within the next two weeks." Sure enough, the Lord answered his prayer within a week.

Some time later, he asked the Lord again to send in people of other races. Then this person showed up. We were excited, but some in the ministry were not enthusiastic, especially when they married someone in the Church of another race. As time went on, they told me they felt some in the congregation treated them differently because of their race. I couldn't believe it, and they could prove nothing. The ones they accused denied they had a problem with their race, and the Lord was quiet on the matter. Unfortunately, no matter how comfortable people tried to make them feel, they still thought they were being treated differently by people in the congregation. Whether it was true was not the issue. How they felt was the issue.

Sadly, there are many minorities hiding prejudices in the Church. And many in the majority group in the Church are racist. Racism in the Church is what drives racism in the community. *"For the name of God is blasphemed among the Gentiles through you, as it is written"* (Romans 2:24). Someone will always seek to segregate communities as long as believers keep Churches segregated. If you desire to see social justice and equality in your community, address the community's belief system.

Jesus said, *"Thou shalt love thy neighbor as thyself"* (Matthew 22:39 b-only). Ask yourself, "Am I genuinely being taught the Doctrine of Love?" The Bible is clear. The Lord is looking at the Church: *"If my people, which are called by my name, shall humble themselves, and pray, and seek my face, and turn from their wicked ways; then will I hear from heaven, and will forgive their sin, and will heal their land"* (2nd Chronicles 7:14).

When the Lord seeks to change a social system, He calls people to repentance. He aims to change people's hearts first. Specifically, He looks at those who say they believe in Him. Whenever I hear an argument for a segregated Church or community, the view is rooted in Old Testament Scriptures. However, in the Old Testament, the Lord did not have a problem with skin color. He did not desire the Hebrews to marry outside of the Hebrew nation because the land's daughters served other gods. His plan was for the Hebrews to be equally yoked together in a covenant of faith and not devil worship. Again, according to the Book of Galatians chapter three, there is no color or nationality in the New Covenant. The Lord only

339

looks at whether a person believes in His Son Jesus Christ, repents of their sins, is water baptized in Jesus' name, and receives the gift of the Holy Ghost. Anything else is a doctrine of hatred, which stems from devils. 1st John 4:20-21 makes it straightforward, *"If a man say, I love God, and hateth his brother, he is a liar: for he that loveth not his brother whom he hath seen, how can he love God whom he hath not seen? And this commandment have we from him, That he who loveth God love his brother also."*

My husband has personal testimonies of supernatural experiences and heavenly visitations. Whenever there is an opportunity to share his experiences, many confess their sins and give their lives to Jesus. Surprisingly, on one occasion, an American couple of another race asked, "Why you?" My husband responded; I don't know why the Lord chose me to experience such things. In the innocence of his character, my husband did not perceive the underlining question. The man replied, "I understand, but why you?" I discerned what he was saying and explained it to my husband. When we discussed it with the man, he confessed he marveled that the Lord would use a Black man that way. I don't know why he was so surprised. After all, the Biblical patriarchs and Jesus were not White men. That is just one example of the many ways believers display prejudices in the Church.

Again, minorities are also guilty of the racial divide in the Church. For example, there is a testimony from someone I know. The Lord gave them a task to bring souls of diversified nationalities to the Church where they attended service. At first, they wondered whether it was of the Lord. Because they stopped to wonder, they did not do what the Lord instructed them. During that time, they never told anyone what the Lord said. So the Lord took it upon Himself to send a Prophet across their path. The Prophet spoke to their specific situation, even the instructions the Lord had already given them directly that no one else knew. And the Prophet told them: *If you do not go and get those souls that the Lord instructed you to get, you shall surely die.*

After that, the person immediately began to get the souls of diversified nationalities and brought them into the Church, thinking that everyone would be happy that souls were being brought into the ministry, but they were not. During that time, the person who brought in the souls realized whisperings were going on in the form of questions like, "What are they doing? What are they doing here?" At first, they did not believe what they heard or thought they heard because they took a double-take. It wasn't that they thought they heard something that they knew they heard, but they didn't believe that it was actually taking place. So they began to inquire of the Lord and received an answer in the form of an open manifestation. It was openly shown when minorities started mishandling the believers of another nationality. It was so bad that the souls could not stay in that Church. With that said, the Lord let them know He would remove them from their presence to the detriment of the minority-majority group. That is discerned spiritually.

If you are in a segregated Church and believe a doctrine that promotes segregation, you need to ask the Lord to show you why it is false. If you seek the Lord for the truth, He will show you the truth. He may have to send someone to you to expound on the subject matter using the Scriptures. If He does, receive the Lord in them; don't look at the person. After He opens your eyes, repent. Then you can start to pray that the Lord opens the eyes of the leaders and then everyone else in the Church so they can repent too. If they are predestinated for eternal life, the Lord will open their eyes to the truth. Only then can the Lord have his way in the ministry and close the racial divide.

Moreover, if you attend a Church that believes in segregation, forgive them. And if someone forced you out of a Church because it is segregated, forgive them and let go of the hurt. Pray for the leaders and the congregation. Pray that they see the error of their ways and place the rest in the Lord's hands. Don't talk about them. Pray! If the Lord gives you the charge to go and tell them their error, do it! And keep praying until you see a change in their hearts. If they do not change, they will be hard-pressed to receive the Kingdom of Heaven. 1st John 2:10-11 declares, *"He that loveth his brother abideth in the light, and there is none occasion of stumbling in him. But he that hateth his brother is in darkness, and walketh in darkness, and knoweth not whither he goeth, because that darkness hath blinded his eyes."*

Reader:

Racism, prejudice, and hatred are serious evil spirits. You may have to cry out to the Lord for a long time to get rid of them. Especially the spirit of hatred, depending on how deeply rooted it is. The spirit of hatred drives racism and prejudices. If you struggle with letting hatred go, it means you also have a spirit of fear. The fear you have may come from an unwillingness to deal with peer pressure and family loyalties. When someone is battling spirits of racism, they usually have acquaintances and family members who support their mindsets and behaviors. Also, people who are fearful of racial equality have difficulty coping with cultural biases. However, if you love the Lord, and for your soul's sake, you will take heed to Jesus' instruction and release those spirits. If you don't let them go, they will increase in power in your life and spread to others, including your children. As long as you continue to operate in those spirits, you will be unprepared for the rapture or your death, whichever comes first. Use the prayer below to approach the Lord concerning your specific situation, and then let the Holy Ghost lead you concerning what to pray afterward.

Abba, Father, in the name of Jesus Christ of Nazareth, I do not desire to perish with the world. I thought I operated in a measure of love that I now realize is not love at all. I confess I do have a problem with people of other races and nationalities. Lord, I know You will not hold my sincerity concerning correcting this matter against me, so I'm asking you to reveal the error of my ways to me so I can confess all my heart to You, no matter how ugly, and repent. Please show me the truth about the spirits of hatred and racism and forgive me for my ignorance. I now realize that in raging against others because of their race, I have been raging against You for a long time, and I'm afraid to see how deep the darkness goes in my character. Nevertheless, I trust you will be with me, so show me where I am in the spirit realm and what you would have me to do concerning this matter. Help me to see all of Your creation as You see them and grant me to love all humanity in the name of Jesus Christ of Nazareth. Amen!

CHAPTER FIFTEEN

THEY HEARD NONE OF MY COUNSEL

"A wise man will hear, and will increase learning; and a man of understanding shall attain unto wise counsels:"

Proverbs 1:5

CHAPTER 15: *THEY HEARD NONE OF MY COUNSEL*

"They would none of my counsel: they despised all my reproof" (Proverbs 1:30). Some of you are hurt because the Lord told you things you shared with someone else, and they didn't believe you. Especially if you are someone who gave a message to an individual or a congregation, and they didn't receive it as a message from the Lord, and you suffered consequences like a physical attack or an attack on your character. As the Word of God promises, it will be required of all believers to suffer for righteousness' sake.

Instead of being angry that they rejected you, remember the Scriptures in the Book of 1st Peter 3:14-17, *"But and if ye suffer for righteousness' sake, happy are ye: and be not afraid of their terror, neither be troubled; But sanctify the Lord God in your hearts: and be ready always to give an answer to every man that asketh you a reason of the hope that is in you with meekness and fear: Having a good conscience; that, whereas they speak evil of you, as of evildoers, they may be ashamed that falsely accuse your good conversation in Christ. For it is better, if the will of God be so, that ye suffer for well doing, than for evil doing."*

Some of you have served as counselors, and the recipient treated you as a crazy person. Or they treated your counsel like it was from someone who had ulterior motives. Some people even dared to say you were of the devil and told others not to listen to you. John 7:17 declares, *"If any man will do his will, he shall know of the doctrine, whether it be of God, or whether I speak of myself."* The main question is not *ONLY* whether the messenger belongs to God, but whether the hearer belongs to God. If the hearer truly belongs to the Lord, they will discern whether the Word spoken is from the Lord or not. But if they refuse to hear and attack the person, then that is saying something too. Either the hearer does not belong to the Lord, or they are guilty of speaking evil over others themselves, and now they fear the same thing is happening to them. There is no one who has the power to speak something into your life or over you that the Lord has to honor or cannot dishonor; consider Balaam in Numbers 22:21-39. The power is not only in the words spoken but in the One True Living God who has to back the words. Besides, if it is not the Lord, and the messenger is not true, then nothing will happen in any wise. Someone who is not called of the Lord to speak to you that thing they are speaking has no authority to do anything against the Lord's will for your life. So, stop attacking the messenger.

Accusations and attacks against your character can be extremely painful. However, those genuinely called of the Lord will suffer these things. You have to remember you are a vessel for the Lord. You are to warn and teach others in wisdom. The Lord will bless those who listen, and those who refuse will miss what the Lord has for them. So we should never take it personally when someone doesn't hear us because they refuse to listen to the Lord, not the vessel. And truthfully, if someone calls you the devil for speaking the Word of the Lord, then it is blasphemy, and the accuser will never recover from blasphemous statements against the Holy Ghost.

In this day and age, the world will physically and mentally attack the Lord's servants more and more for speaking the Word of the Lord. I heard about a Prophetess when she was in her sixties, whom the Lord sent to a Church to declare a Word of the Lord. Instead of hearing the Word of the Lord through her, they dragged her out of the building. During the incident, they left her with scrapes and bruises. It was so bad they did not even let her get her purse. Likewise, a Man of God was sent to a Church to give a Word of the Lord, and he was also dragged out and roughed up in the Church parking lot. Neither of these servants fought back or defended themselves, according to these examples in Scripture: 2nd Chronicles

18:23, *"Then Zedekiah the son of Chenaanah came near, and smote Micaiah upon the cheek, and said, Which way went the Spirit of the LORD from me to speak unto thee?"*

Moreover, Jeremiah 38:4-6, *"Therefore the princes said unto the king, We beseech thee, let this man be put to death: for thus he weakeneth the hands of the men of war that remain in this city, and the hands of all the people, in speaking such words unto them: for this man seeketh not the welfare of this people, but the hurt. Then Zedekiah the king said, Behold, he is in your hand: for the king is not he that can do any thing against you. Then took they Jeremiah, and cast him into the dungeon of Malchiah the son of Hammelech, that was in the court of the prison: and they let down Jeremiah with cords. And in the dungeon there was no water, but mire: so Jeremiah sunk in the mire."* It is scary when Churches today carry on as they did in the Bible, persecuting Prophetic Officers. In the New Testament, even the Apostles were persecuted and killed; *but woe to that man by whom the offence cometh* (Matthew 18:7). The Word of God is supposed to be an example to us, yet some did not get the memo.

The truth is they did not drag a man or woman out of the Church; it was the Lord Jesus Christ they dragged out of the Church. The Word of God declares in John 13:20, *"Verily, verily, I say unto*

352

you, He that receiveth whomsoever I send receiveth me; and he that receiveth me receiveth him that sent me." It is not personal. Church hurt comes about when we take rejection personally. Imagine an entire continent of people not receiving the Lord's servant. From city to city, province to province, state to state, or country to country, the people's overall manner is to reject the teachings the Lord gives them. It can be hurtful, but again you should not take it personally.

On the other hand, many are held in contempt in the Church because, unfortunately, some have made themselves common or familiar. It is difficult enough for people to receive the truth, and if the people are familiar with the vessel the Lord desires to use, it will be more challenging to hear the Lord's instruction through that vessel. Consider, Mark 6:1-6, *"AND he went out from thence, and came into his own country; and his disciples follow him. And when the sabbath day was come, he began to teach in the synagogue: and many hearing him were astonished, saying, From whence hath this man these things? and what wisdom is this which is given unto him, that even such mighty works are wrought by his hands? Is not this the carpenter, the son of Mary, the brother of James, and Joses, and of Juda, and Simon? and are not his sisters here with us? And they were offended at him. But Jesus said unto them, A prophet is not without*

353

honour, but in his own country, and among his own kin, and in his
own house. And he could there do no mighty work, save that he laid
his hands upon a few sick folk, and healed them. And he marvelled
because of their unbelief. And he went round about the villages,
teaching."

Jesus could not help those in His own country because they thought they knew Him. Unfortunately, the townspeople only knew Him as the carpenter's son and not as the Messiah, the Only Begotten Son of the One True Living God! And so shall it be with the Lord's servants. So when someone doesn't hear your counsel, don't take it personally. After all, it is the Lord's words they are rejecting, not yours.

Reader, pray this prayer with me:

Abba, Father, in the name of Jesus Christ of Nazareth, forgive me for being angry with those who did not listen to my counsel. I realize now those who did not receive me did not accept You. Therefore, empower me to kick the dust off my feet and move on to continue Your work, in Jesus' name. Amen!

As I wrote this book, I listened carefully to the Lord concerning what He would have me write. I wrote with as much integrity and discretion as possible, only writing about the situations the Lord would have me to relay. Don't be alarmed if I did not cover your specific Church hurt. The main point of this book is the principle of true forgiveness and the healing that follows. Just understand no matter what you are facing, the Lord knows about it, and you may apply the principles in this book to your life in its current season.

I cannot express the power we receive through our obedience to the Lord. Daily reading of the Bible, prayer, fasting, praise, and worship will also empower you to stand amid a fiery trial. I cannot describe in words the long-term benefits of guarding your heart against congregation life and holding on to the joy you get from the Lord. It is something you have to live to understand. All these things will make you strong in the Lord. I cannot emphasize enough the importance of putting on the whole armor of God and keeping it on. My husband taught the congregation that we do not have to put on our armor every day; just don't take it off. Some days it will be challenging to keep on your armor, but it wouldn't be a battle if it were easy. You are going to have to fight for your salvation and your peace of mind. You will have to *". . . work out your own salvation with fear and trembling"* (Philippians 2:12).

The Lord just told me to share with you all a testimony of several of us women praying for a young lady in the Church. We all thought she was still saved. Apparently, at some point, she took off the **armour of God.** As we prayed, I began to beseech the Lord to forgive her. I told her to start repenting to the Lord. As she was on her knees and we all were praying, suddenly I saw the *Helmet of Salvation* come down from Heaven onto her head. It was about eighteen inches tall and white with gold trim. Unfortunately, within six months, she laid it down again and left the ministry.

When you get things right with Jesus and start to forgive, it will seem like your efforts to forgive and release anger are in vain. You may not see a change right away because human nature is habitual. After the Lord does His part and sets you free, you have to break the habits of talking about the situation and being slow to forgive. But I assure you, if you walk in the Word of God consistently, you will wake up one day and notice you no longer talk about that person or situation. You will see you are more apt to forgive and pray when something happens.

There will be clarity in your thought processes, and you will notice peace in your mind, spirit, and home. You will also have a better understanding of why you faced those particular tests and trials. Moreover, you will see a reversal of the physical effects of your unforgivingness, and you will experience healing in your mind and body. You will also witness a greater level of love and worship toward the Lord, and you will love others more fervently. Your relationship with the Lord will be healthier, and you will find ease in desiring to please Him. Finally, there will be a tangible change in your life to a degree where others will see and inquire about this new you.

Change is not easy. It is not easy to love or forgive. Yet, if you find the courage to do so, you will experience the gracious, compassionate, and merciful nature of the God you serve. However, if you don't forgive and endure what the Lord requires, you will not experience the blessings the Lord has planned for your life.

ABOUT THE AUTHOR

On July 12, 1996, I formally met the Lord Jesus Christ. Upon meeting Him, I confessed my sins and was baptized in water in the name of the Lord Jesus Christ. I committed my life to Him, and nine days later, I was filled with the Holy Ghost, receiving power from the Throne of God. After my conversion, I came to understand that Jesus was there with me my whole life and now has broken chains of oppression that plagued me for years. He also healed me mentally, physically, emotionally, and socially and has supplied all my needs. As of this day, I can say I lack nothing. Jesus Christ is and will forever be my Lord, Savior, and King.

Furthermore, the Lord Jesus has given me the strength to continue laboring beside my husband in ministry for over eighteen years. Although I serve in the capacities of Prophetess, Evangelist, Teacher, Psalmist, and Scribe, I see myself as the Lord's handmaiden. The Lord has also given me the gift of authorship, charging me to write several books by the Holy Ghost's power and wisdom. He empowered me to earn four college degrees. Everything I have accomplished has been by His power. All praises to Jesus Christ, King of Kings and Lord of Lords!

DISSERTATION

A quantitative study of selected predictors of job tenure, job satisfaction, and satisfaction with job promotion opportunity (2015)

BOOKS BY THE AUTHOR

1. *The College Organizer Technique* (E-book) (2009)
2. *Are you really waiting: On God's promise for a divine spouse?* (2010)

CONTACT INFORMATION

Contact the author at *www.ATcicJMinistries.org*

CREDENTIALS

PhD, Capella University, Minneapolis, MN, Dec 2015

MSA, Central Michigan University, Mt. Pleasant, MI, Dec 2010

BBA, Eastern Michigan University, Ypsilanti, MI, Apr 2008

ABA, Oakland Community College, Bloomfield Hills, MI, Aug 2000

PRAYERS AND SONGS

For comforting songs and prayers, go to *ATcicJMinistries.org*

REFERENCES

Applebury. G. (2020a). *Infidelity statistics on men, women, and relationships.* LovetoKnow.com.

https://divorce.lovetoknow.com/Rates_of_Divorce_for_Adult ery_and_Infidelity

Applebury. G. (2020b). *Top reasons for divorce.* LovetoKnow.com.

https://divorce.lovetoknow.com/Top_Reasons_for_Divorce

Betts, J. (2020). *Divorce statistics by religion.* LovetoKnow.com.

https://divorce.lovetoknow.com/Divorce_Statistics_by_Religi on

Blakemore, E. (2019). The Brutal History of Japan's 'Comfort Women'| History.

https://www.history.com/.amp/news/comfort-women-japan-military-brothels-korea

Fisher, H. (2014). *10 facts about infidelity.* Ted.com.

https://ideas.ted.com/10-facts-about-infidelity-helen-fisher/

Grabmeier, J. (2004). *When Europeans were slaves: Research suggests White slavery was much more common than previously believed.* Ohio State News.

https://news.osu.edu/when-europeans-were-slaves--research-suggests-white-slavery-was-much-more-common-than-

previously-believed/

Konchalovsky, A. (Director). (1985). *Runaway train* [Film]. The

Cannon Group, Inc.

Solomon, S.D. & Teagno, L.J. (2018). *Frequently-asked questions

about Infidelity.* Divorce Magazine.

https://www.divorcemag.com/articles/frequently-asked-

questions-about-infidelity

Turvey, C. (2015). *Women more likely than men to initiate divorces,

but not non-marital breakups.* American Sociological

Association. https://www.asanet.org/press-center/press-

releases/women-more-likely-men-initiate-divorces-not-non-

marital-breakups

NOTES

Lightning Source UK Ltd.
Milton Keynes UK
UKHW020901040122
396592UK00014B/670